ROBERT K. MERTON

KEY SOCIOLOGISTS

Series Editor: PETER HAMILTON
The Open University, Milton Keynes

This series presents concise and readable texts covering the work, life and influence of many of the most important sociologists, and sociologically-relevant thinkers, from the birth of the discipline to the present day. Aimed primarily at the undergraduate, the books will also be useful to pre-university students and others who are interested in the main ideas of sociology's major thinkers.

MARX AND MARXISM
PETER WORSLEY, Professor of Sociology, University of Manchester

MAX WEBER
FRANK PARKIN, Tutor in Politics and Fellow of Magdalen College, Oxford

EMILE DURKHEIM
KENNETH THOMPSON, Reader in Sociology, Faculty of Social Sciences, The Open University, Milton Keynes

TALCOTT PARSONS
PETER HAMILTON, The Open University, Milton Keynes

SIGMUND FREUD
ROBERT BOCOCK, The Open University, Milton Keynes

C. WRIGHT MILLS
J. E. T. ELDRIDGE, Department of Sociology, University of Glasgow

THE FRANKFURT SCHOOL
TOM BOTTOMORE, Emeritus Professor of Sociology, University of Sussex

GEORG SIMMEL
DAVID FRISBY, Department of Sociology, University of Glasgow

KARL MANNHEIM
DAVID KETTLER, Professor of Political Studies, Trent University, Ontario; VOLKER MEJA, Associate Professor of Sociology, Memorial University of Newfoundland, and NICO STEHR, Professor of Sociology, University of Alberta

MICHEL FOUCAULT
BARRY SMART, Department of Sociological Studies, University of Sheffield

THE ETHNOMETHODOLOGISTS
WES SHARROCK and BOB ANDERSON, Department of Sociology, University of Manchester

ERVING GOFFMAN
TOM BURNS, Emeritus Professor of Sociology, University of Edinburgh

JÜRGEN HABERMAS
MICHAEL PUSEY, University of New South Wales, Australia

ROBERT K. MERTON
CHARLES CROTHERS, University of Auckland, New Zealand

ROBERT K. MERTON

CHARLES CROTHERS
Department of Sociology
University of Auckland, New Zealand

ELLIS HORWOOD LIMITED
Publishers · Chichester

TAVISTOCK PUBLICATIONS
London and New York

First published in 1987 by
ELLIS HORWOOD LIMITED
Market Cross House, Cooper Street,
Chichester, Sussex, PO19 1EB, England
and

TAVISTOCK PUBLICATIONS LIMITED
11 New Fetter Lane, London EC4P 4EE

Published in the USA by
TAVISTOCK PUBLICATIONS
and ELLIS HORWOOD LIMITED
in association with METHUEN INC.
29 West 35th Street, New York, NY 10001–2291

British Library Cataloguing in Publication Data
Crothers, Charles
Robert K. Merton. — (Key Sociologists).
1. Merton, Robert K.
I. Title   II. Series
301'.092'4   HM22.U62M3/
Library of Congress CIP data available

ISBN 0–7458–0122–6 (Ellis Horwood Limited — Library Edn.)
ISBN 0–7458–0123–4 (Ellis Horwood Limited — Student Edn.)

Phototypeset in Times by Ellis Horwood Limited
Printed and bound in Great Britain by Richard Clay Limited, Chichester, W. Sussex

Table of contents

Charles Henry Gardner Crothers has been Lecturer (1983–85), and is now Senior Lecturer (1985–) in the Department of Sociology, University of Auckland, New Zealand. He was previously Senior Research Officer (Social Planning) at the Town and Country Planning Division, Ministry of Works and Development, Wellington (1978–82), and Junior Lecturer in the Department of Sociology, Victoria University of Wellington (1975–78). He was awarded a B.A. (1968) in Geography from the University of Waikato; a B.A. (Hons) (1970), and a Ph.D. (1978), both in Sociology from the Victoria University of Wellington.

Editor's foreword

As a sociologist Robert Merton stands at a crossroads between the great sociologists of the late nineteenth and early twentieth centuries, and the professional or institutionalized sociology of the present day.

His work and his academic career bridge two rather different styles of sociological expression. The first has as its role models Max Weber, Georg Simmel, Emile Durkheim, Pitirim Sorokin, Karl Mannheim, and their disciples or followers. It is a European model, rooted in social and cultural contexts in which the typical sociologist was an upper-middle-class intellectual concerned with an elite and esoteric form of knowledge. As a style it contrasts strongly with the 'mass-sociology' of the second half of the twentieth century, a subject used by and familiar to large numbers of students and others throughout the Western world, but given perhaps its highest form of expression in the American university system. This second, and heavily Americanized style of sociological expression, is both a child of the explosion of higher education in the post-Second World War world, and a major tool of the planning process in Western societies, which has seen the provision of such educational facilities as an indispensible step towards constant and maintained economic growth.

In the European form of sociology, the emphasis is almost always on the conceptual schema used to understand society and its structures. Since the object of sociology was essentially to provide a commentary or critique of social phenomena, to an audience whose interests were for the main part intellectual rather than practical, the elegance or scope of the 'grand theory' was preeminent. Its scientific validity was not the primary object of concern, and it was not designed to be applied to practical issues or problems.

Merton was one of the first modern sociologists to recognize the significance of the connection between the scientific validity of sociological theory and its practical role as a tool for resolving social problems, in their widest sense. As Charles Crothers makes clear in his careful examination of Merton's influence on modern sociology, his role has been one of directing a significant proportion of the professionalized and institutionalized sociology during its period of major and far-reaching growth — essentially from the 1950s until the 1970s.

The distinctive and fascinating aspect of Dr Crothers's treatment of Merton's work lies in his delineation of an emergent 'general theory' within the emphasis on 'theories of the middle range' for which Merton is so justly famous. Because Merton did not appear to be championing a 'grand theory' of classical but esoteric dimensions like his teacher and colleague Talcott Parsons, he has not attracted the partisan and factional critiques which have so obscured a measured and objective assessment of the Parsonian theoretical canon.

Nonetheless, and despite his disavowal of 'grand theory', Merton's influence on contemporary sociology is perhaps significantly greater than Parsons's. Dr Crothers provides the best and most accessible account of the development of Merton's work, focusing both on his role as 'discipline builder', and on his contributions to various important sub-disciplinary fields (science, medicine and deviance stand out), in a commentary that is both lucid and original.

As we progress further towards the next millennium the future of sociology seems assured, as an indispensable discipline for understanding and adapting to the rapid and unsettling pace of social change. Whilst sociology has not yet become a wholly 'respectable' discipline, the seriousness with which its more scientifically grounded propositions are now taken is in very large part due to the strategic role played by Robert Merton in the development of modern sociology. Dr Crothers's book will be essential reading for anyone who wants to understand the key nature of Merton's contribution to contemporary sociology.

Peter Hamilton

Epigraph

. . . The limits of Merton's work derive in part from its essentially 'liberal' bathos . . . These limits do not derive only from Merton's liberal side but also from his 'rebel' side . . . , that is, Merton's limits derive as much from the rebel horse he rode, as from the liberal snaffle and curb with which he held it in check. . . . In passing a serious judgement on Merton's work . . . it should be seen historically, in terms of what it meant when it first appeared and made the rounds. . . . Merton's work on anomie . . . was a liberative work, for those who lived with it as part of a living culture as distinct from how it may now appear as part of the mere record of that once-lived culture.

There are several reasons for this. One is that Merton . . . kept open an avenue of access to Marxist theory. . . . Merton was much more Marxist than his silences on that question may make it seem. Unlike Parsons, Merton always knew his Marx and knew thoroughly the nuances of controversy in living Marxist culture. Merton developed his generalized analysis of the various forms of deviant culture by locating them within a systematic formalization of Durkheim's theory of anomie, from which he gained analytic distance by tacitly grounding himself in a Marxian ontology of social contradiction. It is perhaps this Hegelian dimension of Marxism that has had the most enduring effect on Merton's analytical rules, and which disposed him to view anomie as the unanticipated outcome of social institutions that thwarted men in their effort to acquire the very goods and values that these same institutions had encouraged them to pursue. In its openness to the internal contradictions of capitalist culture few Lukacians have been more incisive.

(Gouldner, 1973, pp. x, xi; this note included contrasts with C. Wright Mills which have been deleted as they seemed unnecessary for present purposes.)

Acknowledgements

I would like to thank several colleagues for reading part or all of my manuscript and/or for discussing issues arising from this study: Kit Malagoda, Georgina Murray, Nick Perry.

Peter Hamilton has provided distant encouragement; Robert Merton helpfully supplied several fugitive references and patiently answered an array of factual questions; and Mei Everitt typed the script.

Dedications

This study is dedicated to Robert K. Merton. I hope that it captures the style and thrust of his work, and perhaps provides a sketch of the overview he never presented.

Secondarily, I would like to indicate my great debt to Arthur Stinchcombe for having seen so deeply into the latent general theory at the heart of Merton's approach and for the wider group of Mertonians and even anti-Mertonians (spanning such a diverse grouping as Lewis Coser, David Caplovitz, Alvin Gouldner and Randall Collins) who have explored, developed or criticized his thought.

Note on sources

Almost all the significant writings by Merton have been assembled in four volumes (with a very slight overlap in content). *Social Theory and Social Structure* was first published in 1949 with subsequent editions in 1957 and 1968. Each edition retains a four-part structure:

— on theoretical sociology (on relations between theory and research, and functional analysis);
— studies in social and cultural structure (anomie, bureaucracy and reference groups);
— sociology of knowledge and mass communications;
— sociology of science.

The 1957 edition includes four extra essays (two of which are 'continuities' that attempt to update analyses included in the first edition) which expand its volume by one-third, and it also incorporates some revisions. The 1968 edition differs from its predecessor only in a very considerable expansion of its introduction into two chapters.

All references in this study to material from *Social Theory and Social Structure* are to the 1968 edition (although the date when an essay was first published is also indicated when this is important in establishing a chronological sequence). Similarly, where this is possible, reference is always made to the version of any article which is available in one or other of the four volumes, and this is indicated by square brackets in the citation.

Another 13 essays are gathered from symposia and journal articles into the 1976 collection (1976b), *Sociological Ambivalence*. Several of these essays provide analyses of sociological ambivalence (which involves examining the stresses arising for individuals out of contrasting aspects of the social structures they are embedded in), while other essays deal with a wide variety of theoretical issues, and a final set with ethnic relations.

In 1973 most of Merton's work in the Sociology of Science was assembled by Norman Storer into a volume with the same title. This volume also includes much of Merton's work in the sociology of knowledge. Storer provides a useful introduction and prefatory notes for each part, that sketch the background of, and develop themes within, Merton's sociology of science. The volume has five parts:

— The Sociology of Knowledge;
— The Sociology of Scientific Knowledge;
— The Normative Structure of Science;
— The Reward Structure of Science;
— Processes of Evaluation in Science.

A further selection is reproduced in *Social Research and the Practising Professions* (1982a) edited by Aaron Rosenblatt and Thomas F. Gieryn, who also provide a useful introduction. This volume seeks to relate Merton's analysis of the social organization of (social) science to his analysis of professions, and also to reprint some of his essays on the interaction between the two; it is therefore organized in three parts:

— Sociology of Social Research;
— Sociology of the Practising Professions;
— Social Research Applied to Public Policy.

An interesting feature is the construction by the editors of a "composite form" of Merton's essay on 'Social Problems and Sociological Theory' from the 1961, 1966, 1971 and 1976 editions of *Contemporary Social Problems*. (However, a closer textual examination of this reveals that several useful analytical points made in the 1976 edition are not included in this version.)

The more important books and articles in Merton's extensive bibliography are included in the select bibliography at the end of this book. A full listing up to 1975 has been published (Miles, 1975) and an update is available (Miles, 1985). The more important and useful secondary writings are also included in the bibliography (see also the listing of commentaries, continuities etc. of Merton's works in Miles (1975, 1985) and in the bibliographies assembled in several 'continuities' sections of *Social Theory and Social Structure,* in the bibliography attached to the 1970 reprinting of *Science, Technology and Society in Seventeenth Century England* and in

Storer's edition of *Merton's Sociology of Science,* 1973). Secondary writings on Merton are extensive and scattered, but relatively few provide useful exegesis or criticism: I have tried to winnow out only the more relevant rather than attempt an exhaustive catalogue. Some of this material is available through the *Festschrift* edited by Lewis Coser (1975a), through reviews of this, and also through a second but much less useful *Festschrift* edited by Gieryn (1980). Collins (1977) is critical of the generally positive stance taken by contributors in the Coser volume, but it is a valuable source precisely because of this. The second collection comes from a more remote set of commentators (American sociologists were excluded) and is thus somewhat disconnected from the main thrusts of Merton's work. Clinard (1964) is a collection debating the success of Merton's 'anomie theory' to that point in time.

Details of Merton's personal biography are sparse, as he has received direct attention only in Hunt's (1961) portrait in the *New Yorker,* a brief discussion between Coser and Nisbet (1975), an account of his teaching style commissioned by *Teaching Sociology* (Persell, 1984), and an interview (published in Italian) on his current theoretical work on "socially expected durations" (De Lellio, 1985). Other biographical material is almost entirely based on Hunt's article. However, Merton has himself published some attempts to document the 'career' of some of his projects (including a postscript to his essay on intermarriage [Merton, 1976], an extended personal memoir on the development of the sociology of science [Merton, 1977]) and also accounts of his working relationships with colleagues (Lazarsfeld [Merton, 1979b], Parsons [Merton, 1980b], Gouldner [Merton, 1982b], Znaniecki [Merton, 1983] and Sarton [Merton, 1985a]).

Since the writing of this book began, a book on Merton by Piotr Sztompka (*Robert K. Merton: an intellectual profile*; 1986) was announced by Macmillan, but it was not yet available by the time this study was sent to press. The description of this book indicates that Sztompka, too, sees Merton as a general theorist and, in addition, Sztompka sees Merton as 'the last classical sociologist'. Without seeing the supporting argument it is difficult to comment, although it seems to me rather that Merton straddles classical and contemporary sociology, with his roots in the former, but with his concerns for scientific cumulation strongly centred in the latter. To some extent it might be argued, along with Ben-David (1973, 1978) that he has largely worked in a mode intermediate between the two. Given Merton's own work on 'multiple discoveries' it is perhaps ironic that, after at least a decade when there has been little general attention to Merton's work, there should be a more-or-less simultaneous 'discovery' of its general significance.

1

The case for examining Merton

1.1 PROBLEMS IN STANDARD ACCOUNTS OF 'STANDARD AMERICAN SOCIOLOGY'

The theoretical grounding of many contemporary 'European' social theorists lies with the 'founding fathers' (Marx, Durkheim, Weber) and the complexly intertwined threads of exegesis and extension that stretch forward from them. The transmission-line of major theoretical ideas seems to mainly bypass those early and mid-twentieth century decades in which the development of sociological knowledge was largely left in American hands. And yet during these years of the American custody of sociology's conceptual storehouse, a range of conceptual developments were constructed that still have important roles to play in contemporary sociology. But many contemporary British and 'European' social theorists have very considerable difficulty in relating to, and being able to use, this American offering. Often, attempts are made by these theorists to weld Weberian revisions into a Marxian framework, which almost unconsciously smuggle in American concepts to accomplish this task. The tendency for an unknowing functionalism to lurk largely undetected behind many arguments is now well-attested (e.g. Alexander, 1982; Blau, 1975b, Gouldner, 1973b; Sztompka, 1974).

Even North American sociologists have considerable difficulty in conceptualizing the history of their own contributions to sociology. Many of the available accounts contradict each other and often involve somewhat idiosyncratic and not particularly successful typologies. Once various early American theorists have been treated and the 'Chicago School' described, treatment of the sociology of the 1950s and 1960s often falters. This is largely because individual thinkers are replaced by wider networks of scholars working collectively within broad traditions. The tools of theoretical exegesis in sociology seem rather too blunt to easily handle these broader developments and make adequate sense of the period.North American sociology of the post-war period is usually characterized using one or other, or both, of two labels —'structural-functionalism' and 'empiricism' (cf. Eisenstadt and Curelaru, 1976; Freidrichs, 1970; Gouldner, 1970; Mills, 1959; Mullins, 1973; Shils, 1970).

The theoretical arm of post-World War II American sociology is often seen as a 'grand theory', which took a 'structural-functionalist' form, and which was detached from both empirical concerns and social criticism. Under the apparent theoretical aegis of Talcott Parsons, a complex and terminologically dense conceptual framework is seen as having developed a conservative social theory during the 'end of ideology' decades of the 1950s and 1960s. This approach is depicted as seeing social order as emanating from socialized conformity to cultural ideas, with a self-righting, equilibrium-seeking social system quickly restoring any departures from the status quo.

The other arm of post-war American sociology is often seen to involve an 'abstracted empiricism' wherein micro-problems about the explanations of the social distribution of attitudes and behaviour were relentlessly attacked by a myriad of social survey studies, without sufficient concern for understanding the structural anchoring of these social minutiae in wider social contexts. Instead of developing theoretical explanations, intellectual effort is seen as being deflected into polishing methodological niceties. This partially collective social psychology is seen as holding a 'positivist' philosophy of science in which the facticity of the social world is held to be unproblematic, so that a scientific derivation of 'laws' can be developed, in which the purity of freedom from moral commitments or concerns is defended by a doctrine of value-freedom. Yet worse, this 'value-free' empiricism is seen as being pressed into the service of the ruling class and the state in a social engineering role, that attempts to neatly remedy any blemishes without challenging the whole.

While this dual image of the post-war development of American sociology expresses a considerable grain of truth, it has difficulties in accounting for much of what the sociological development of the post-World War II decades involved. Certainly, rather more was going on in American sociology in this period, and it was rather more significant than this generally received account suggests. (As another commentator briefly queries after a similar depiction of American sociology, "I am not convinced that this is the whole truth about American sociology in this period . . ." (Bryant, 1976, p. 19).)

The picture must be immediately widened to include the 'loyal opposition' of symbolic interactionism, and its associated qualitative field research methodology, which throughout the period was held to be particularly cherished by the scattered remnants of the older 'Chicago School'.

But the degree of polarization posited in this picture that American sociology covers both 'grand theory' and 'abstracted empiricism' creates further and more significant difficulties. How could such diverse tendencies be incorporated within a single (or even within the dominant) sociological tradition? I think it is plausible to argue that Parsonian grand theory was in fact a relatively separate cognitive development, borne by a narrow theoretical 'sect', which had relatively little direct influence on the development of American sociology. Nevertheless, the indirect influence was clearly considerable, as the network mapping of Mullins (1973) shows. Talcott Parsons's theoretical writings were used in particular as an umbrella under which the status of sociology as a theoretically orientated discipline could be sheltered. His work, too, was at least partially absorbed into the 'textbook culture' which undergirds the teaching enterprise aspect of sociology. And, Parsons reflected (as Sorokin, 1966, pointed out) much of the general conceptualizing of the time, and could then be used as a scholarly legitimation of this. But, his direct influence on sociological theorizing and research was perhaps far more limited than is often held. After all, his work did not lead to the ready development of research problems or the easy formulation of theoretical explanations.

The rising methodological sophistication of social research work and the more formal couching of theoretical models that characterized post-war American sociology cannot be easily dismissed as being only concerned with trivia. Its general attractiveness, as it spread around the world, was based on a perceived explanatory potential that many critics of its moral tone failed to grasp, and that its own advocates were not adequately able to articulate. If Parsons's grand theory was difficult to draw on, and since a 'proper' functional mode of explanation was only relatively rarely deployed (see Davis, 1959), the theoretical ideas used must surely have been drawn from some source. A close study of the rhetoric used to establish explanations in post-war American sociology is needed to ground this argument. It seems to me that Merton would be found in such an investigation to have played a crucial shaping role in the development of sociology over this period. This study is devoted to arguing this case.

1.2 PROBLEMS IN ACCOUNTING FOR MERTON'S ROLE IN 'STANDARD AMERICAN SOCIOLOGY'

The putative importance of Merton's contribution is reasonably obvious. Apart from Talcott Parsons, he is the only other American social theorist of a general stature in that era. Beyond Merton there is a scatter of important sociological writers — Coser, Gans, Goffman, Gouldner, Nisbet, Barrington Moore, etc. — but none seems to have sufficient stature, and to have sustained a sufficient depth of analysis, to have influenced a broad sector of sociological work. This general argument for the predominant influence of Parsons and Merton compared to other sociological writers of the period can be backed up by published personal testimony of major textbook writers (see below), and also by citation studies (Bain, 1962; Cole and Zuckerman, 1975; Cole, 1975; Garfield, 1977, 1980; Menzies, 1982; Mullins, 1973; Oromaner, 1968, 1970, 1980; Wells, 1979; Wells and Picou, 1981; Westie, 1973 [putting this range of studies alongside each other in a listing, of course, hardly implies that there is a detailed consensus in their findings]).

The logic of my argument might seem to press on to leave Merton holding centre stage in 'standard American sociology', since I have already argued that Parsons's role is rather more complex and slight than is usually understood, and that there are no other clear rivals in sight. But this position, too, is both simplistic and fallacious. I am content merely to establish a *prima facie* case for the very considerable importance of Merton's work in the development of American post-war sociology. Clearly other factors, and many other influences were at work.

Given this central importance of Merton, it might be expected that the general sociological implications of his work would have received detailed critical attention. After all, Talcott Parsons has attracted a bevy of commentators, and C. Wright Mills has been lionized or lambasted in several publications. Yet, although there are several major areas of sociological debate in which Merton's work features prominently, the analysis of Merton's general approach to sociology is slight, both in quality and quantity. There are a few, mostly brief, chapters on Merton in theory texts (e.g. Abel, 1970; Bierstedt, 1981; Coser, 1977; Cuzzort, 1969; Loomis and Loomis, 1965; Mulkay, 1971; Turner, 1974; Wallace, 1969, 1983) and a scattering of critical articles (in general, see Bibliography). In these Merton is usually portrayed as a structural-functional loyalist, differing only in minor detail (not least in graciousness of writing-style!) from the grand master. Even the more detailed of these accounts cover only highly selected portions of Merton's work, and are concerned more to describe than to analyse how he constructs his analyses. Some texts explicitly deny that ". . . he has produced a systematic theory or a system of sociology" (Bierstedt, 1981, p. 445).

The two *Festschriften* dedicated to Merton (Coser, 1975a; Gieryn, 1980) very largely contain papers by peers or students which direct little attention to the general elucidation of his ideas, and as is appropriate for such volumes, seem to have been used by them as a platform on which to enunciate particular themes (often extensions of Merton's work) rather than to provide the opportunity for overall and critical evaluation: compare the evaluation contained in Firth's critical collection on Malinowski (Firth, 1957) or the treatment of Sorokin (Allen, 1963). Several of those chapters in the two *Festschriften* which do directly attend to his work are more concerned with measuring its impact through citations than in elucidating the internal logic of its conceptual structure.

There are several explanations of this relative neglect. Merton's own writing is clear and direct, and does not draw attention to the need for developing interpretative commentary. This is reinforced by Merton's explicit methodological doctrine of 'middle-range' theory which deflects attention from his own general theory-building (see Stinchcombe, 1975).

But there may also be psychosocial mechanisms at work that have acted as barriers to closer attention. To his own generation Merton was doubtless a 'prophet in his own land', to be cited only where particularly relevant, and to the succeeding generation his work was to be used rather than inspected. And he is not yet ancient enough to be extensively mined for historical work. There was no particular occasion in which broader examination was called for, and perhaps there is a structural resistance arising out of master–apprenticeship and similar scholarly patterns (cf. Merton, 1963a). This ambivalence towards a preceding intellectual generation is nicely pointed up in the Preface to Stinchcombe's *Constructing Social Theories*: "Robert K. Merton was another classic writer who ranked with Durkheim, Marx and Trotsky in my earlier intellectual life. I have been a bit bewildered by his becoming a contemporary as I grow older" (1968, p. vii).

1.3 STRUCTURE OF ARGUMENT

This study is concerned with trying to unscramble a difficulty in the recent history of sociology, which involves the gap between the apparent and the actual influence of Merton. On the one hand, Merton clearly had a considerable impact on American sociology as recognized by those he influenced. Indeed, I have argued that this impact may well have been quite considerably greater than that of Parsons or other social theorists of his era. But, it is difficult to pin down, in the absence of any depth of critical literature, what it is exactly about his writing and work that might account for his influence. The rather rag-bag and severely limited treatment by textbook commentators of Mertonian doctrines such as 'middle-range theories', or the 'paradigm of functional analysis', or 'patterns of anomie', or 'unintended consequences' suggests that there is little consensus on what the main features of his work are, and little appreciation of its overall architecture. Nor are Merton's own comments on his work much help: as when *Social Theory and Social Structure* was declared a citation classic Merton (1980c) merely enumerates some of the areas of work it contains — reference-groups, local and cosmopolitan influentials, the self-fulfilling prophecy, unanticipated consequences, the paradigm of the sociology of knowledge, and sociology of science — without reference to any underlying theme.

The social theorists that one finds attractive appeal at an intuitive level, and it is the task of commentators on theory to make explicit these attractive features. In my own gut-level feeling, perhaps the most salient theoretical feature about Merton's theorizing is his concern for, and skill in providing, fine-tuned structural analyses that build around a fairly straightforward but nicely angled idea. So often his analyses seem 'to work', they seem to 'get things right'. In particular, his analyses of how social structures work and how they impinge on patterns of behaviour are so often provocatively clear. This orientation in his work is enhanced by the careful way in which he sets up problems for sociological analysis and the clear self-conscious style in which he develops his theories, and the modest, open-ended nature of his approach. If this intuitive feel that many have about the analytical payoffs in Merton's writing is correct, then we should try to pin down exactly how he goes about producing such analyses.

The general thrust of my approach to understanding Merton's work is two-fold. One arm is built around Hunt's (1961) observation that Merton was widely regarded as a central figure largely uncontaminated by sociology's many squabbling factions. Similarly, Turner (1974, p. 73) remarks that "His tempered and reasoned statements have typically resolved intellectually stagnating controversies in the field." (This is a different — but not markedly different — interpretation from the more usual image that Merton clasped closely to the centre of the dominant 'structural-functional' paradigm.) I shall argue that Merton had a central role in sociology as a 'discipline-builder', especially in setting research agenda, and in shaping the methodological stances suited to studying these questions. His role has been reinforced by the central organizational positions he has held.

The second arm of this argument builds on Stinchcombe's (1975) insight that Merton's own emphasis on 'middle-range theorizing' has blinded us, as well as Merton himself, to the fact that he has actually built up a flexible and powerful analytical framework that actually is a general theory. Despite the protests against general theory that spring from his own methodological doctrines, Merton does contribute a general social theory. This general theory can be recovered by careful examination of the complete array of his general writing and more specific studies (through a symptomatic reading

— cf. Turner, 1981, p. 8). My rendition of this underlying general theory attempts to both amend and extend Stinchcombe's essay.

These two mutually reinforcing lines of argument occupy the three main chapters of this study. They are preceded by a standard treatment of Merton's 'intellectual career' and the influences which have shaped it, and followed by a selected treatment of Merton's specialist work in particular fields — especially deviance, and the sociology of science. This treatment of his more specific work is intended to deflect little from my main concern, which is to uncover the general model of analysis underlying Merton's work. Rather, this chapter on Merton's substantive analyses will mainly reinforce this concern by showing how the more general model is drawn on in tackling more specific topics, and it also picks up on the more trenchant criticism his more specific work has attracted (compared to the less incisive reaction to his more general approaches). The penultimate chapter outlines some of the criticisms that have been made of his inattention to major questions in macrosociology and the moral implications of his understated ethical stance. The final chapter attempts a review of the value of his general sociological approach. The Epilogue brings together the haunting ironies which thread through the writing of this study.

1.4   AIMS AND LIMITS OF STUDY

Merton has drawn a careful distinction between the 'history' of social theory and its 'systematics' (1948a[1968b, Chapter 1]), and has derided the frequent conflation of the two in many 'theory/history of theory' texts. This study must confront the question of which of these two categories it falls into. I have, so far, justified my interest in Merton's work in terms of its intrinsic interest, and the relative rarity of critical and comprehensive examinations of it, and more widely because I think that understanding Merton's approach to sociology is central to understanding the strengths and weaknesses of American post-war sociology. This may seem, at first blush, a rationale for a study in the history of social theory. And this study does include such an aspect, incorporating snatches of a sociology of Merton's sociology. But its main concern is the systematics of theory. After all, sorting out the cognitive structure is surely a prior task, which must be tackled before the historian can trace through the affiliations of ideas and examine the social influences which may have shaped the construction of the cognitive structure. And this study is concerned with systematics in another direction: I feel that Merton's approach and his analytical schema are still fresh and valid, and both are significant building bases for contemporary social analyses. In particular, this study intends to point up some of the constraints and dilemmas involved in carrying out the tasks of developing any social theory, using Merton as a case study.

In order to attempt a critical rather than a definitive study, several limitations have had to be imposed. It is not necessary, or even appropriate, to indulge here in invidious comparison of the alternative impacts of Parsons and Merton (a position also adopted in Coser, 1977, p. 567), although I am not necessarily convinced that a close examination would favour the conventional picture of Parsons's dominance. Their relative impact at the theoretical level is open to argument, but I would support Coser's opinion, also shared by Stinchcombe (1975, p. 11) that " . . . there is little doubt that Merton's theoretical stress on problems of the middle range has been more pronounced in its impact on empirical research than has the Parsonian grand theory" (1977, p. 567).

Similarly, any temptation to trace the detail of debates and criticisms into the murky depths of the more distant parts of the secondary literature had to be resisted. Silence on some points does not imply that I am not biting my tongue through the lack of space for some decidedly argumentative footnotes.

The largest lacuna in this study is that it is based solely on Merton's published work and does not attempt to come to grips with either the ongoing front of theoretical developments which remain 'orally published', or the very considerable back-territory of material available only in typescript or semi-published form. Nor have I sought to incorporate Merton's own views on his work. While these limitations (although 'limitations' seems hardly the most well-chosen term!) at least make the present task more manageable, they do condemn this study to remaining a preliminary attempt at an overview.

2

Merton's intellectual biography

2.1 BIOGRAPHY

Merton's formal biography is relatively straightforward. He was born in 1910 in Philadelphia. In 1927 he won a scholarship to Temple University and ·in 1931 a fellowship to Harvard University for graduate work in sociology. In 1932 he gained a Harvard M.A., and he began his doctoral dissertation, completing this in 1935; and in 1936 became an instructor and tutor at Harvard. In 1939 he was appointed as associate professor and then professor at Tulane University, New Orleans, serving as chairman of the department. In 1941 he became assistant professor at Columbia University, New York, being subsequently promoted to associate professor (1944) and full professor (1947), and succeeding Lazarsfeld as Chairman of the Department in 1961 for several years.

In 1963 he was appointed Franklin Henry Giddings Professor of Sociology; in 1974 he acquired the rank (shared by only three others at Columbia) of 'University Professor'; and from 1979 he has been 'Special Service Professor' and 'University Professor Emeritus'. From 1942 to 1971 he served as Associate Director in the Bureau of Applied Social Research.

Professional activities have included the Presidencies of the American Sociological Association (1956–1957), the Eastern Sociological Society (1968–69), the Sociological Research Association (1968) and the Society for Social Studies of Science (1975–76). Honorary degrees have been given by some 20 universities including Temple, Emory, Leyden, Western Reserve, Colgate, Yale, Wales, Chicago, Pennsylvania, Harvard, Jerusalem, Maryland, Brandeis, State University of New York, Columbia and Oxford. (It is significant that Merton's honour from Oxford — not an institution renowned for its hospitality to sociology — is a Doctorate of Letters rather than Philosophy.) Merton has been a Fellow of the Guggenheim Foundation (1962–63) and the Centre for Advanced Studies in Behavioral Science and has been both Resident Scholar at the Russell Sage Foundation and Adjunct Professor at the Rockefeller University since 1979. Prizes have been awarded him by the American Council of Learned Societies, the National Institute of Medicine, the American Academy of Arts and Sciences (Talcott Parsons Prize for Social Science), the Memorial Sloan-Kettering Cancer Center, Society for Social Studies of Science (Bernal Award), American Sociological Association (Common Wealth award and Career Distinguished Scholarship award) and, perhaps most prestigious of all, he has been a MacArthur Prize Fellow (1983–1988). He has also held numerous advisory posts across a range of social science, humanities and scientific areas.

2.2   SOCIAL CONTEXT OF BIOGRAPHY

It is possible to flesh out the stark details of the formal biography to a degree using published information, but this may only throw a faint degree of light on his career. Much of this background comes from a particularly useful profile written by Hunt (1961) for the *New Yorker,* which paints the following vivid *journalistic* account of his early life and his scholarly style of work (mainly as paraphrased in *Current Biography* (1965)).

Robert King Merton was born on July 5, 1910, in Philadelphia, Pennsylvania, the second of two children of immigrants from Eastern Europe. His father scraped out a living as a carpenter and truck driver, and Merton grew up in the slums of South Philadelphia. Although he took part in the street fights of his neighbourhood as a member of a juvenile gang, he was also hungry for learning — a hunger he often satisfied at the local public library. By the time he was eight years old he was reading in all fields, but his favourite was biography. At twelve he became an amateur magician who performed for money at neighbourhood social functions.

Upon his graduation from the South Philadelphia High School for Boys in February, 1927, Merton won a scholarship to Temple University, where he soon established himself as a brilliant student. In his freshman year he majored in philosophy and became a protege of James Dunham, the dean of Temple and a professor of philosophy, but he switched to sociology in his sophomore year, after he had taken an introductory course in the subject from a young and enthusiastic instructor, George E. Simpson. Eventually Merton became Simpson's research assistant and he recalls that his dedication to sociology intensified when he experienced "the joy of discovering that it was possible to examine human behaviour objectively and without using loaded moral preconceptions".

When Merton received his B.A. degree from Temple University in 1931, he was honoured with a fellowship for graduate work at Harvard, where he took full advantage of the opportunity to study with such distinguished professors as Talcott Parsons, George Sarton, Pitirim Sorokin, and L. J. Henderson. For a time he lived on something like $500 dollars a year, subsisting on a diet of sandwiches, milkshakes, and his own manufactured whiskey . . . .

Robert King Merton married Suzanne M. Carhart, a social worker whom he met when she was a student at Temple University, on September 8, 1934, soon after he was appointed as an instructor at Harvard. They have a son and two daughters. Although he is tall and lean and is austere and clerical in appearance, Merton soon dispels an initial impression of solemnity, and his associates, friends and neighbours know him a convivial man with a wide range of interests and a flair for brilliant conversation. A tireless worker and a perfectionist in whatever he undertakes, he . . . gets up as early as 4.30 in the morning to tackle his many professional projects . . .. He is an independent in politics. Critical of his own work, he sometimes takes years to finish an important project and release it to the publishers . . . .

What Merton does in his study after four-thirty every morning is to evaluate, classify, and abbreviate into notes the masses of material derived from his own readings and from surveys, interviews, and tabulations made under his direction by a dozen graduate students. Picking out some item . . . he studies it, pauses to puff on his pipe and stare meditatively at the ceiling, then turns to a battery of ten staggeringly cross-indexed filing cases containing the thousands of figures and millions of words he has compiled over the last twenty-five years and rummages through one of them for a document to compare with the paper before him. Having drawn some conclusion from the comparison, he jots a few notes on a pad, looks up a handful of obscure allusions, computes a quick mean deviation or chi-square analysis, and rattles off his findings on a typewriter, using paper of three different colors for extra-special cross-referencing.

It would be possible to flesh out a few more incidents in the social background to Merton's life from published material (for example, the way illness has stalked his life: he lists sprue, Meniere's syndrome, Dupuytren's contracture, a gangrened appendix, pneumonias and cancer (Merton, 1982, p. 924) or the fact that his children at one stage festooned his household with 15 cats, with both children and secondly the cats being the subject of the dedication of *On the Shoulders of Giants*). Other glimpses of the Faculty at Columbia can be gleaned from Lipset's (1955) account of the department, autobiographies from MacIver (1968), Lipset (1969b) and Page (1982), and Horowitz's (1983) biography of C. Wright Mills. However, it may be appropriate to dwell only on the most crucial status-passage in his career, when in 1941 he joined first the Columbia faculty and then the Bureau of Applied Social Research.

Merton's 'joint' appointment to the Columbia faculty with Paul Lazarsfeld was a fortunate accident. When a full professorship fell vacant in 1940 the Department was split between Robert Lynd and Robert MacIver and could not agree on a nomination. A compromise was effected by the University President (Nicholas Murray Butler) who split the position into two assistant professorships — one emphasizing social theory and the other empirical research. Merton was appointed to one, and Lazarsfeld to the other. For a while the two had little contact, but then followed an intellectual seduction. Lazarsfeld invited Merton and his wife to dinner but diverted him to his research enterprise on audience-testing a government pre-war morale-building radio programme.

> After the program, when an assistant of Lazarsfeld's questioned the audience on the reasons for its recorded likes and dislikes, Merton perked up; he detected theoretical shortcomings in the way questions were being put. He started passing scribbled notes to Lazarsfeld . . . . As a second batch of listeners entered the studio, Lazarsfeld asked Merton if he would do the post-program questioning. Merton did . . . . (Lazarsfeld, 1975, p. 36)

Thereafter, Merton became engaged in work with the emerging Bureau of Applied Social Research, supervising projects and becoming a co-director. Both worked at the Bureau, and Lazarsfeld would nobble Merton in the late afternoon and early evening for discussions (in Bureau idiom "scheming sessions") in which ways for improving studies and developing the Bureau were explored. The collaboration proved fruitful over the long run in ways that the later Parsons–Stouffer theory–methods combination at Harvard never managed to achieve (Coleman, 1972, pp. 400, 401).

2.3 PERFORMANCE IN THE ARRAY OF SOCIOLOGIAL ROLES

It was appropriate to organize the above fleshing out of Merton's biography using the notion of a status-sequence. This next section will briefly examine

Merton's performance in various of the array of roles available to the status-occupant of any university teaching/research position: as scholar, editor, 'lover of words', reviewer, teacher, organizer, consultant and social critic (cf. the list given by Merton, 1973, pp. 519–522).

2.3.1   Scholarship

It is difficult, amidst the maze of different editions and reprintings (see Miles, 1975, 1985), to exactly pin down the dimensions of Merton's scholarly output, but its characteristics in outline are:

— 12 books
— 11 edited books
— 125 articles
— 120 book reviews (Persell,1984).

He has also been a compiler of several series of reprinted books. As with Parsons (Hamilton, 1983, p. 44) Merton had his early books published by the Free Press, a new firm which actively published sociological work. His work has been widely translated (for example, *Social Theory and Social Structure* has been translated into a dozen languages) and frequently reprinted (for example, 'Social Structure and Anomie' has been reprinted some 40 times. Besides, this " . . . for all his publications, Merton has a writing block" (Caplovitz, 1977, p. 143). He has several unpublished book manuscripts and many unpublished paper drafts, many in the form of notes for teaching or conference presentations. Indeed, Merton (1980a) has drawn attention to the importance in his work, and that of others, of the advancing front of 'oral publications' which often precede printed scholarly form. But Merton has also been careful to avoid publication of unworthy material, and has not regretted some of his 'non-publication'.

Merton usually presents his work in the form of an essay, a form of writing over which he exhibits consummate control. It is probably fairly easy to recognize the particular style of a Mertonian essay, but it is rather more difficult to distinguish analytically its key characteristics. Merton departs from more austere forms of essay-writing in that he deploys headed sections and uses listings, emphases, tables and other devices to enumerate points or to point up interrelationships. Another hallmark of his writings is an abundance of reference notes (as opposed to Parsons's sparse use of references) designed " . . . to place American sociology . . . in the mainstream of worldwide scholarship [since] Merton wrote in an intellectual climate in which sophisticated scholarship could not be taken for granted" (Coser, 1975b, pp. 89, 90).

However, the dense thicket of historical and contemporary references seems sometimes diverting, and even Coser pointedly remarks that Merton's abundant footnoting has a 'functional autonomy' of its own!

Coser's codification of the ways in which Merton attempts to relate his work to the European tradition is also a useful general picture of his essay-writing approach:

> When choosing a problem for investigation, Merton seems most of the time to have been stimulated by (1) a public issue that was salient at the time; or by (2) a theoretical formulation by a previous thinker . . . ; or by (3) general scholarly interest in a particular area of inquiry. The execution of the project, in turn, led him to either (a) use previous scholarship to buttress his argument; or (b) use that scholarship in order to suggest formulations, refinements and reformulations; or (c) use that scholarship to suggest new lines of inquiry (Coser, 1975b, p. 91).

Merton is very careful in his attribution of concepts and terms to predecessors, at the risk of being accused (see Sorokin, 1966) of merely repeating the work of others. Yet Merton seldom uses any concept without imparting to it a novel twist.

Besides his theoretical essays, Merton has also variously been involved in the proposing, design, execution and (occasionally!) publication of a range of empirical projects and also some work in the codification of methodology.

Merton has frequently worked closely with collaborators and research assistants (often, it appears, wives of colleagues). Beyond his immediate working environment, Merton has been particularly supportive of other scholars, drawing widely on their work and providing encouragement. Merton has seldom engaged in any extended polemic or even exchange of views, although from time to time he has firmly and carefully commented on the work of others where he has felt it was insufficiently scholarly. Dahrendorf, Dubin, Feuer, Mills, Mitroff, and others, have been subject to vigorous critique without rancour. However, Merton has been quite reluctant to enter the lists in defence of his own work. In this he is consistent with his own arguments (the 'kinder cole' principle: Merton, 1965) about the distorting effect of public polemics amongst scientists.

One difficulty with Merton's writings is that over time many of his pieces have been revised, often without explicit signposting. Many papers have been worked up orally in lectures or seminars, presented as a conference paper, published in a major journal and then included in several editions of *Social Theory and Social Structure*. While this practice shows Merton's commitment to the ongoing reworking and extension of his work, it can be a difficulty for scholarship, with confusion arising as commentators use different versions.

2.3.2 Editing

A major, but largely invisible, role that Merton discharged has been his close and active editing of other scholars' writings. Caplovitz argues that these tasks of reading and commenting have taken up much of Merton's professional life, and have severely cut into his own publishing performance.

> Merton became engaged as an editor in four different ways. Early in his career, he was frequently asked by publishers to evaluate manuscripts that they were considering publishing. Second, he edited the papers of the various contributors to collections of essays that he edited, notably *Sociology Today* and *Contemporary Social Problems*. Third, some twenty-five years ago he became the sociological editor for Harcourt Brace and thus evaluated all the social science books they considered publishing; and finally he receives each year a large number of unsolicited manuscripts from former students and colleagues for his opinions of their work (Caplovitz, 1977, p. 146).

Caplovitz notes that an early publisher's request was, at the suggestion of Franz Neumann, to evaluate Sweezy's *The Theory of Capitalist Development*. Other manuscripts criticized in detail include James West's *Plainville, USA*, Wilbert E. Moore's *Industrial Relations and the Social Order*, Robert MacIver's *Social Causation*, Kingsley Davis's *Human Society*, Alfred Kroeber's *Anthropology* (second edition), Theodore Caplow's *The Principles of Organization*, Alvin and Helen Gouldner's *Modern Sociology* and Matilda White Riley's *Sociological Research: a case approach* (Caplovitz, 1977, pp. 147, 148).

The extensive scattering of thankful notes for Merton's editing comments in authors' Prefaces ranges from Talcott Parsons in his *Structure of Social Action* (1937) to Anthony Giddens's *The Constitution of Society* (1984).

Much of Merton's contribution in 'close' editing work lies in offering reformulations of and additions to arguments, as well as in showing how prose can be sharpened or highlighted and needless words omitted. Merton's 'rough' editing works to clear up and structure the presentation of arguments (Caplovitz, 1977). His editing for Harcourt Brace Jovanovich — as well as of many other books — often involved highlighting and summarizing key themes through an introductory preface. However, Merton appears in his editing work not to attempt to restructure the writer's manuscript along lines that suited his own theories, although undoubtedly many of his comments were based on his own work. Instead, he clearly has a great ability to work into the author's own lines of argument. But this very ability to blend in with the formulations of other writers may have lessened the extent to which his editing work aided the development of his own work.

2.3.3   Reviewing

Merton was very active as a book reviewer, especially early in his career, many written as part of a series. Most of these have been straightforward descriptive and critical notices, but in several (e.g. 1941b) Merton has actively summarized and developed the author's material.

2.3.4   'Lover of words'

A particular quality of Merton's writing is his love, akin to a poet's or philologist's, of words and language (Caplovitz, 1977). This interest in words is a concern to sharpen and highlight concepts with evocative terms, and not the usual poet's attempt to point to a meaning with subtle and complex imagery. In this respect, his terminology has a vividness that sharply contrasts with the dullness of Parsons's prose. Many of these terms are recovered from archaic usage, a practice enhanced by his favourite reading, which Caplovitz tells us is " . . . not the ASR or AJS, but rather those eighteenth and nineteenth century literary magazines, *The Edinburgh Review, Notes and Inquiries* and *Athenaeum*" and because "he is a fond collector of rare books that he uncovers in-out-of-the way second-hand bookstores" (Caplovitz, 1977, p. 144). Hunt (1961) provides an extended description of one example of Merton's writing style:

> Many of Merton's writings, furthermore, are liberally flavoured with apposite references to literature and history. An introduction he wrote to an anthology called *Sociology Today* either quotes or alludes to John Aubrey, Charles Darwin, Herbert Spencer, Seneca, Descartes, Hegel, and John Stuart Mill, and another of his books, *Mass Persuasion*, is sprinkled with choice morsels from Thomas Hobbes, Plato, Aristotle, de Tocqueville, Julian Huxley, and Kate Smith.

This love of words further extends to the coining, or more usually recovery, of some splendid terms. This has often been highly successful. His resurrection of the richly evocative term 'serendipity' in the field of sociology has been taken up by the discipline and the media. In a paper on the drift of sociological ideas into the vernacular, Merton has supplied a list of his own neologisms:

> . . . self-fulfilling prophecy, manifest and latent functions, the displacement of goals, retreatism (a social phenomenon become widely known a generation later as 'opting out'), opportunity-structures, role-sets and status-sets, local and cosmopolitan influentials, the Matthew effect, accumulation of advantage, theories of the middle range, homophily (friendships between people of the same kind, not as more recently proposed, a synonym for homosexuality) and heterophily, strategic research site, obliteration by incorporation, potentials of relevance and the acronym OTSOG (standing for the title of a book of mine, *On The Shoulders of Giants* . . . : 1982a, p. 102).

Several of his accounts (and especially several unpublished ones) have explored the history of use of a particular aphorism — most notably the supposedly Newtonian phrase "If I have seen further, it is by standing on the shoulders of giants" (1965), and also the changing use of the term 'serendipity'.

His interest in words spills over into the occasional use of poetry (sometimes suitably paraphrased for the purpose at hand) to drive home a particular point, and into a severely controlled scholarly wit (perhaps most clearly expressed in his little "Foreword to a Preface for an Introduction to a Prolegomenon to a Discourse on a Certain Subject": 1969). Merton's erudition has been supported by his command of several languages — French, German and Italian. However, this facility has not been accompanied by an oral fluency, which in earlier days restrained a possible interest in study overseas (De Lellio, 1985).

2.3.5   Teaching

Merton has taught a variety of courses and seminars, but since going to Columbia, only at graduate level (Persell, 1984). While some of his minor and shortlived options have included race relations and cities, most attention was devoted to courses in the theory of social control (up to the mid-1950s) and structural analysis. Besides these lecture formats, he was involved with seminars on particular topics (in earlier days, some offered with Lazarsfeld) and more recently seminars in the sociology of science with Harriet Zuckerman.

In his course on social control Merton " . . . took all the giants of the discipline and showed how the work of each complemented that of others and how the whole constituted a theory of social control" (Caplovitz, 1977, p. 142). The other course, on the 'Analysis of Social Structure', was the seedbed for Merton's own theoretical developments. It was first taught in 1937 at Harvard under the title 'Social Organization', and continued at Columbia for several decades.

> Apart from the [50] odd students registered in these courses, the classroom would be packed with auditors. Many of the auditors would return year after year. The reason that auditors would return year after year was because these courses were living things, continuously evolving. Before each lecture, Merton would spend several hours preparing his presentation for the day. He always managed to evolve new ideas and insights that gave his lectures a freshness in spite of his many years of lecturing on the same topics. Because he was so deeply involved with his own insights and developing thought, Merton managed to convey his intellectual excitement to his students (Caplovitz, 1977, p. 142).

This dynamic quality of Merton's teaching was even more important in seminar formats in which there was much interaction. He deliberately chose to use these formats as a self-conscious way of developing and testing ideas in the course of their public presentation.

Many of Merton's publications flowed from his teaching. Several key papers were rapidly published from his Harvard theory course, and others from his ethnic and race relations course at Tulane. However, later, while at Columbia the lag between oral and formal publication widened — with Merton estimating the modal gap at 11 or 12 years (Persell, 1984, p. 364). It is likely that this teaching approach was at least partly influenced by Parsons's teaching style, given the similarity Merton reports in "Remembering the Young Talcott Parsons" (Merton, 1980b). For many academics, their research interests are centred around their teaching duties; Merton has been in a position to allow his general interests to shape his teaching.

2.3.6 Organizing

Cole and Zuckerman note various organizational efforts Merton made in developing the sociology of science as a specialty, as he " . . . encouraged the scheduling of sessions at ASA in the early 1960s, by agreeing to chair them or to prepare papers, and was one of the chief organizers of the ISA Committee [the International Sociological Association's Research Committee in the Sociology of Science]" (1975, p. 164). But they go on to comment that Merton does not find these activities congenial. He does not want to organize things or to run them. Unlike his teacher, George Sarton, who avidly devoted himself to establishing an elaborate organizational infrastructure for the history of science, Merton has set about most of these tasks reluctantly and has been far less effective than Sarton (1975, pp. 164, 165).

Nevertheless, Merton has been prominent in a range of efforts to secure the infrastructure needed to underpin the development of social science research (for example, his active encouragement of Eugene Garfield's Citation Indexes).

Merton early was placed in an informal leadership role; for example, with Horowitz's biography of C. Wright Mills casting him as mediating, through correspondence, between Gerth and Mills (Horowitz, 1983). Merton's letter files undoubtedly would reveal a mesh of correspondence that helped informally to pull together much of the American and world sociology establishment.

2.3.7   Consulting

Lazarsfeld (1975) mentions that Merton engaged in consulting, especially in relation to the Bureau of Applied Social Research, but only traces of this have surfaced in the published literature. (The account by Merton and Devereux (1964b), summarizes a larger storehouse of material.) His later work as consultant to the American Nursing Association has led to several short useful essays (see 1982a) that explore areas of occupational and organizational sociology relevant to nursing (together with a footnoted admonition that improvement in the economic and social status of nurses might require wresting of at least some power away from doctors!)

2.3.8   Social criticism

Although, as Hunt reports, Merton preferred to take an 'independent' political position, this has not precluded him from some involvement in liberal causes. Examples of this include neighbourhood- and national-level involvement in civil liberties issues and supporting the President of a public TV station who was being dismissed (Merton's intention to be the moderator of a social, cultural and political programme for the station lapsed with this incident: see Hunt, 1961).

2.4   PHASES OF INTELLECTUAL CAREER

Merton's research and writing programme can be divided into five phases, which approximate to the various decades of his academic working life —

the 1930s, 1940s, 1950s, 1960s and 1970s (and to his own age-periods — his 20s, 30s, 40s, 50s and 60s). However, as with any such schema, this is approximate, and is used only to provide a general framework for understanding the progression of his interests, and the relationships amongst its various phases. This brief chronological account is supplemented in Chapters 4, 5 and 6 by consideration of the content of his work.

Merton's main interests have lain in social theory and the sociology of science and knowledge, but subsidiary interests also covered the sociological areas of deviance, ethnic relations, social research methodology, urban sociology, mass communications, professions, medical sociology, complex organizations, and the sociology of social research, including relationships with policy makers. Fig. 1 indicates periods of concentration.

Field of study	*Phases* (and approximate decade)				
	I (1930s)	II (1940s)	II (1950s)	IV (1960s)	V (1970/80s)
Theory	xx	xx	xx	xx	xx
Science	xx	x	x	xx	xx
Knowledge	x	xx		x	x
Methods	x	xx	x		
Deviance	xx	x	x	x	
Ethnic relations	x	x			
Urban sociology		x			
Mass communications		x			
Professions		xx	x	x	
Medical			xx	x	
Organizations		x	x		
S. of Social Research		x	x	x	

Key:

xx = major concentration

 x = some work

Fig. 1 — Phases of Merton's intellectual biography.

2.4.1 "1930s"

Before his own writing and research began Merton had been well-schooled in then-contemporary American sociology. He saw the 1921 textbook – treatise *Introduction to the Science of Sociology* by Park and Burgess as consolidating concepts about social processes, and in so doing incorporating much material from European sociology (1964a, p. 214). Besides this he became involved while at Harvard in intensive reading of European sociology, including the systematic scouring of French sociology which he wrote up in his first publications (Merton, 1934a, 1934b).

On the empirical side he was involved in a series of research studies (see Hunt, 1961) that included work as an undergraduate on Simpson's (his instructor in sociology at Temple University) research study on references to Negroes over some decades of Philadelphia newspapers, and then, at Harvard, fieldwork amongst the homeless of Boston, and several laborious library projects developing long-term quantitative indicators of changes in science, technology and medicine (Merton, 1977, pp. 24, 25). Finally, his own doctoral work involved quantitative analyses of shifts in the foci of scientific interests, and shifts in the occupational interests of the English elite which involved hand-tabulating six thousand biographies, and the experiments recorded in the *Transactions of the Royal Society*. These studies involved content analysis and 'prosopography' (i.e. collective biography), both research procedures that Merton usefully helped to transfer into the sociology of science. Although the doctoral work was published soon afterwards (1938a), it remained trapped in the specialist history of science literature — not even obtaining a review in the *American Journal of Sociology* until some thirty years later (Nelson, 1972) — and had almost no general impact within sociology.

A secondary interest in this period involved theoretical work, especially in the sociology of deviance, which largely flowed out of teaching tasks and the developing theoretical concerns of the small sociological community at Harvard. This work involved an essay on the "Unanticipated Consequences of Purposive Social Action" (1936b) and the essay on "Social Structure and Anomie" (1938b). These essays were important for sketching out a more general sociological stance, and had a far-reaching impact within sociology.

Merton's work in this early period also involved some review work on other aspects of European sociology, a structural (and functional) analysis of inter-caste marriages (1941b) and work on the social background factors affecting educational success (1944). (Although this latter work was competent if not particularly evocative it could have been seen as an interesting precursor to the later work on social mobility developed particularly by Blau and Duncan: yet Merton does not grasp the opportunity to link the empirical study to the interest in the American Dream of social mobility he exhibited in his 'anomie theory', for which these data might have been relevant.)

2.4.2 "1940s"

The "second" phase of work in the 1940s had two main sources — material based on several empirically based studies arising from research projects carried out in the Bureau of Applied Social Research at Columbia University and the development of theoretical and methodological stances continuing from his work of the previous decade.

Several of the earlier of these Bureau projects arose out of war-related work, and much of the remainder of his attention was focused on a major comparative community study which was linked to a contemporary trend for large-scale 'planned community' housing developments. Of those studies which he carried out, the one he drew on most was a multi-method study of the effectiveness of a campaign in which a radio star (Kate Smith) hosted a marathon war-bond drive (1946). This study is interesting (see Lazarsfeld, 1975) for the centrality it accorded the imputation of 'sincerity' to a motherly radio figure by listeners who, in a mass society, felt they lived in a world riddled with deception and pseudo-Gemeinschaft ("the feigning of personal concern with the other fellow in order to manipulate him the better" (1946 [1971, p. 142])). This is another theme more recently taken up by cultural critics.

In addition, Merton participated in (and indeed co-edited) an extensive review of various empirical studies sponsored by the American army during World War II, teasing out and developing Herbert Hyman's neglected theory of 'reference groups'. These were largely studies carried out by teams. Merton's immediate interests lay less in carrying through practical study reports than in working out significant methodological or theoretical aspects.

His methodological interests during this period included several aspects of fieldwork involved in community studies (1947b), and the methodology of 'the focused interview' (1956). His theoretical interests included reference-group behaviour (1950) and later, the social processes of friendship formation (1954).

In addition to this work on projects, Merton assembled the various writings that constituted his composite theoretical and methodological stance within sociology and which formed the themes of *Social Theory and Social Structure* published in 1949. This included work on the methodology of functional analysis and the interplay of theory and research, and the selection and arrangement of much of the array of theoretical writing and commentary he had produced to that point.

Social Theory and Social Structure is claimed to be particularly concerned with developing, in a systematic unfolding, two pervasive sociological concerns: " . . . the interplay of social theory and social research, and — the concern with codifying both substantive theory and the procedures of sociological analysis, most particularly of qualitative analysis" ([1968b, p. vii]).

2.4.3 "1950s"

The 'third phase'in the 1950s includes a broad programme, which had a higher theoretical emphasis and less explicit methodological concerns than his previous set of work. A wider sponsorship for the programme is sought, and there is more concern to gain resources and recognition for the continued development of sociology as a discipline.

In developing a rationale for the keypiece in this programme — a comparative study of medical education at Cornell University and several other medical schools — Merton identified five convergent developments:

(1) The marked and cumulating interest in the sociology of professions which includes, as a major component, studies of professional schools;
(2) The growing utilization of social science as composing part of the scientific basis for the provision of health care in contemporary society;
(3) The considerable recent growth in the empirical study of complex social organizations, among which schools constitute an important special class;
(4) The similar growth of interest in the process of adult socialization . . . ;
(5) The recent advances in methods and techniques of social inquiry which make it possible to examine these subjects and problems by means of systematic inquiry. (Merton, 1957a [1982a, p166])

Although these developments are presented as convergences relevant to this particular study in the sociology of medicine, this listing also largely represents Merton's own personal research programme over this period. Much of this work built directly on studies carried out through the Bureau of Applied Social Research at Columbia, the large graduate training programme at Columbia University, and interaction with other sociologists in the expanding graduate faculty. Merton's own work in each of these areas, included (in terms of his own numbering above):

(1) A seminar on professions and a planned book (which was never published, although it helped focus later work in this area, especially Columbia commentary by Goode and by Etzioni on types of occupations, limits to the professionalizing strategies of occupations and the characteristics of semiprofessions).
(2) Several essays on the sociology of social research.
(3) A Columbia seminar on complex organizations which led to an edited volume that pulled together a range of classical writing and contemporary empirical research on bureaucracy, and to an informal research

programme that developed a Mertonian/Columbian model of the dysfunctions and workings of complex organizations (especially in the work of Philip Selznick, Alvin Gouldner, and Peter Blau).

(4) Understanding of adult socialization was particularly attempted through a study of the social process of medical education at several (prestigious) medical schools which were in the throes of redesigning their curricula.

(5) A continuing interest in the methodology of social research was shown in the publication of Merton's World War II work on methodology of *The Focused Interview* (1956).

This catalogue shows that Merton's own work was slotted into each of the main components of an emergent framework of concerns in sociology. I think that his work in this period is largely undergirded by a very lightly spelled out macrosociological perspective on modern societies in which its key social forms are identified as professions, bureaucracies, cities and the media. This viewpoint presages the latter postindustrial' imagery developed particularly by Daniel Bell. Merton's work within this framework was not theoretically well-developed, but actively sought to lay out an agenda of issues and then to mobilize theoretical and especially empirical research work around these.

In this period Merton also continued his work on updating and extending various of the theoretical essays laid down in the previous period in a series of 'continuities' and these were included in a much-expanded version of *Social Theory and Social Structure* published in 1957. Indeed, this was a period of considerable theoretical development. As he later commented:

By the mid-50s my own research programme, as distinct from that of the local thought-collective of which I was a member, had shifted from a monographic focus on particular sets of empirical sociological questions to a renewed focus on identifying problems in structural sociology. (1984a, p. 279)

Merton's development of 'role-set' theory was worked up in this period. Work on the properties of groups was facilitated by examination of this area by a seminar of graduate students with a reading programme on Simmel's writings (Levine *et al.,* 1976; Merton, 1968b, p. 364, fn. 46).

At this stage in his career Merton played an important role in developing two major texts that brought together much of then-contemporary American sociology. These were *Sociology Today* (1959: which comprised a set of some two dozen chapters each of which attempted to lay out the significant sociological analytical problems and the state of the art in addressing these concerns for each of a range of specialist areas) and *Contemporary Social Problems* (1961 [1976a]: which reviewed the relationship between social issues and sociological knowledge). These cooperative intellectual enterprises, under Merton's active coordination (the first brought together during his Presidency of the ASA), sought to further map out and identify the analytical roots of Merton's long-term programme for the development of sociology, and to express his own implicit macrosociology.

2.4.4   "1960s"

Merton's 'fourth' phase of work, beginning in the late 1950s and extending through the 1960s, is marked by a noticeable restriction in the span of his writing interests, and a concentrated return to his 'first love' — the sociology of science. This return was staged on the highly visible occasion of his Presidential address to ASA (1957).

Whereas his earlier (1930s) work in the sociology of science had focused on the interrelationship between the social institution of science and other areas of society, Merton's later sociology of science centred on the key internal features of science as an institution. Central to this image of science was the idea that scientific discoveries were, in principle at least, multiples (likely to be uncovered by any of many competitors) and that the reward systems of science impel scientists to seek recognition of their discoveries by others in the form of citations which acknowledge intellectual debts. As a result of the fateful conjunction of these two principles, much of the energy of scientists becomes expended in attempting to secure their property rights to public recognition of their discoveries — if necessary, through occasionally clamorous 'priority disputes'. If the pressure for discovery is too great, social pathologies in science may result.

Much of his work from the late 1950s was in the Columbia Programme in the Sociology of Science supported by the National Science Foundation with his colleagues Harriet Zuckerman, Stephen Cole, Jonathan Cole, and later Thomas Gieryn. This programme included empirical studies of the evaluation systems across several scientific disciplines, of age-structures and the differential effects of codification in science.

Merton also published an empirical study (couched in a delightful Shandean mode) — *On the Shoulders of Giants* (1965: republished as a vicennial edition in 1985) — of the historical trajectory of the uses of this metaphor over time. This has some links to his more formal analysis of science as the "shoulders of giants" aphorism is a key metaphor through which the scientific norm of humility is expressed; but the main message of the book emphasizes the non-linear development of scientific concepts.

During this period Merton also attempted to come to terms with broadening streams in the development of sociology — both through his sociological accounts of social theory (presaging the later sociology of sociology developed by Gouldner (1970) and Friedrichs (1970)) and through theoretical restatements, in which he signalled the importance of recognizing 'sociological ambivalence' that is generated by social structures (1963a).

Alongside these two major foci of interest there continued a stream of tasks associated with being a prominent figure in American sociology, especially providing commentaries and forewords, and updating previously published material. A third, and final, edition of *Social Theory and Social Structure* was produced in 1968.

2.4.5   "1970s"

The 'fifth' phase of the 1970s, and through to the present, covers much in a reminiscent vein — often in the form of obituary material for colleagues he has outlived — together with some rearguard action defending parts of his earlier writings against recent criticism, and some writing tasks which flow from his 'elder statesman' position. During this period there has been a further flowering of Merton's contributions to belles lettres as a humanist as well as a social science scholar. Merton's reminiscent material is often interesting in fleshing out the social background to various parts of his intellectual career, and this is enlivened by his publication of portions of his correspondence. (This involvement in reminiscence and rearguard defence was a position also shared by Talcott Parsons in his last years as a scholar. Indeed, Merton's younger age and greater longevity have allowed him to "play Engels to Parsons' Marx", in presiding over the memories of the 'functional' school.) However, theoretical interests have continued, with Merton signalling a change in emphasis from a preferred 'functional analysis' mode to a 'structural analysis' approach (1975a), and developing his work on 'socially expected durations'(1984a).

2.4.6   Research trajectory

It would be a characteristically Mertonian question to consider: what led to these changing foci of interest? (see Merton, 1938a [1970a, p. 6]). Unfortunately, detailed reconstruction is difficult without supplementing the limited published material. Coser (1975, p. 88, and also Bierstedt, 1981, p. 444) has applied Isaiah Berlin's image of the 'fox' ("who knows many things") to describe the complexities of Merton's research strategy (as opposed to the hedgehog "who knows one big thing" approach that he characterizes as Parsons's strategy). Clearly, there have been complex threads of opportunistic reaction to possibilities made available and also strong guidance from continuing theoretical and methodological themes. The skeins are less entangled at the beginning and then again at the end of his research career — the early focus on sociology of science, and the later return to this. In between there is a growing confidence in reacting less to opportunities which were made available, and instead using his growing prestige in generating research resources to pursue programmes of more central sociological interest. The pressures on prominent scholars from "intellectual entrepreneurs" can be considerable, as witnessed in Merton's 1982 "Self-emancipation Proclamation" that he would no longer tie himself to deadlines not of his own making.

A related question would be to consider whether Merton had notably changed his theoretical approach in tune with any phases in his research trajectory. For the most part, there has been relatively little change, since his basic sociological orientation was clearly laid down during the first decade of his writing and all its basic features can be discovered within his early set of essays and investigations. However, there have been changing emphases: the self-conscious concern with functional analysis dominated his "1940s" period, while by the "1970s" he worked under a "structuralist" label. Another change seems to have been the social psychological approach more often involved with Bureau of Applied Social Research studies in the "1940s" which was complemented in several essays during the "1950s" with a more conscious 'social structure' level of analysis. Lazars-feld detected a shift in the tone of Merton's writing, noting that in the early essay on the intellectual in the bureaucracy no sympathy is shown the latter, and that "the balanced tone of later papers is still absent" (1975, p. 37).

Throughout his career, Merton has worked with a strong emphasis on the long-term development of sociology. This has been accomplished through a variety of particular programmes and through a varied interaction with a broad range of sociologists. There has often been a reluctance to finally commit himself to a definitive statement on sociology generally, or even in any of the specialist areas he has worked in. This reluctance is evidenced in his preparedness to take the active advice of others (Storer, Rosenblatt and Gieryn) in collecting his material into books and Hunt's perceptive comment that:

His friends hope he will soon settle down to the magnum opus they feel he is capable of producing — an integrating work, which will weave the scattered strands of theory into a sturdy fabric. On good days, Merton thinks that some of his unpublished manuscripts are the beginnings of such a work; on bad days he is glumly certain that nothing of the sort can be written by anyone for at least fifty years. (1961, p. 62).

2.5   INTELLECTUAL HERITAGE: INFLUENCES ON MERTON

Merton has established his own official intellectual lineage in the Acknow-
ledgments to his *Social Theory and Social Structure* ([1968b]) where he
thanks:

Charles Hopkins (his brother-in-law, friend and teacher);
George Simpson (his undergraduate teacher);
Pitirim Sorokin (his graduate teacher);
George Sarton (historian of science and early sponsor);
Talcott Parsons (graduate adviser and colleague);
Paul Lazarsfeld (Columbia colleague).

His comments on two of these are worth quoting in full:

Before he became absorbed in the study of historical movements on the
grand scale as represented in his *Social and Cultural Dynamics,* Pitirim
A. Sorokin helped me escape from the provincialism of thinking that
effective studies of society were confined within American borders and
from the slum-encouraged provincialism of thinking that the primary
subject-matter of sociology was centred in such peripheral problems of
social life as divorce and juvenile delinquency (1968b, p. xiii).

In recent years, while we have worked in double harness in the
Columbia University Bureau of Applied Social Research, I have
learned most from Paul F. Lazarsfeld. . . . Not least valuable to me has
been his sceptical curiosity which has compelled me to articulate more
fully than I might otherwise have done my reasons for considering
functional analysis the presently most promising, though not the only,
theoretical orientation to a wide range of problems of human society.
And above all, he has, through his own example, reinforced in myself
the conviction that the great difference between social science and
social dilettantism resides in the systematic and serious, that is to say,
the intellectually responsible and austere, pursuit of what is first
entertained as an interesting idea (1968b, p. xiv).

But these are only his 'masters-at-close-range': much of Merton's concern
was, as Coser puts it a " . . . self-conscious effort to ransack the whole
house of European erudition ..." (Coser, 1975b, p. 89). Whereas Parsons
focused clearly and deeply on a very limited range of European theorists,
Merton draws very widely but less systematically on a very wide array of

European social theorists, many minor, but including several neglected by Parsons — Simmel, Marx and Mannheim (cf. Coser, 1975b, p. 88). Of all these European social theorists, Merton himself chose Durkheim as a role model, especially in respect of following his open-ended train of inquiry across a scatter of topics. Besides Durkheim, Coser identifies Weber, Mannheim, Simmel and Marx as major sources drawn on by Merton. Durkheim was a major source in the development of the anomie theory of deviance, the functional mode of analysis, and more generally Merton's methodological approach; Weber in developing the 'Merton hypothesis' of the religious impetus to the development of seventeenth century science and in work on bureaucracy; Mannheim in sociology of knowledge; Simmel on work on group properties; and Marx for a concern about the operation of class. The ideas of Pareto were exposed through the Henderson seminar at Harvard, which Merton attended along with Parsons, but did not attract (Coser, 1977, p. 424). Yet, Merton wrote systematically on the thinking of none of these classic theorists (apart from Merton's early review essay on Durkheim, 1936b). Rather, each was actively used and reformulated in developing an approach to a particular theoretical problem.

Although Merton's use of earlier American theorists is less remarked (cf. Coser's attention to Merton's use of the European sociological tradition), he also drew on American sociological thought. For example, Gouldner notes *inter alia* ". . . the extremely fruitful uses to which Robert K. Merton has put such classic theorists as C. H. Cooley, H. Spencer, W. G. Sumner, and above all, G. Simmel, in his recent essay on 'Continuities in the Theory of Reference Groups and Social Structure'" (Gouldner, 1973 [1958], pp. 387, 388). Further sources have been Anglo-American social anthropology (Linton, Malinowski and Radcliffe-Brown, Murdock), contemporary sociology, and a range of historians and social critics (for example, the second *Festschrift,* organized by Thomas Gieryn for the New York Academy of Sciences, includes a selection of ". . . scholars and scientists other than American sociologists, whose work [Gieryn] knew Merton to admire" (1980, pp. vii, viii). Gieryn goes on to describe the list of contributors as including: ". . . three sociologists; two based in England and one in Israel. The seven Americans come from eight disciplines: economics, physiology-and-medicine, psychology, philosophy of science, information science and statistics — and — history of science" (1980, Preface). Although the 'Frankfurt School in Exile' inhabited the New School of Social Research on the Columbia campus during the early 1940s and despite Merton's involvement with Lazarsfeld in advising on the "Authoritarian Personality" research, there seems to be have little direct theoretical influence.

The range of influences on Merton, or rather the sources he used, can be illustrated by listing those appearing frequently in the Name Index of *Social Theory and Social Structure* (see Table 1).

2.6   INTELLECTUAL LEGACY: INFLUENCES FROM MERTON

Merton's influence on contemporary sociology is broad and pervasive. In this, it repeats the shape of the pattern of influences on him. Although Merton has worked with a range of collaborators on a sequence of projects, and his work has inspired a series of research programmes, he has not attracted a general school of followers, or even a small sect of devotees as Parsons did (apart perhaps from his close colleagues at Columbia: Harriet Zuckerman and Jonathan Cole).

His influence has broadly affected much of what Mullins (1973) has termed 'Standard American Sociology', and within this the particular current of the 'Columbia School'. Broadly, this characterization involves a conception of a Columbia–Harvard axis, ranged against 'the loyal opposition' of a continuing 'Chicago School' and more generally against those streams of sociology stressing the history of social theory, social criticism, empiricism and commentary on social problems. Pinning down the key characteristics of Standard American Sociology and of its specifically Columbia mode is more difficult: but would generally be held to involve a contemporary focus, a functional theoretical approach locating social phenomena in their social structural contexts, an interest in developing theory, a sophisticated empirical research approach, a considerable degree of moral and political detachment. The differentiation between the Harvard and Columbia variants would generally be seen as relatively minor, and largely involving differences in the preferred mix of theory and research, and in the level at which theory is couched.

The Columbia School is seen as a joint product of both Merton and Lazarsfeld. Throughout the 1940s, 1950s and 1960s Merton played a major role as both a graduate teacher in training a large cohort of sociologists and as an editor in helping shape through editing a wide range of the sociological writing from this group and more generally other sociologists. Columbia was a central seat from which to influence much of the mid-century development of sociology. Besides this university base, Merton was also able to extend his impact using such command over professional resources as he obtained through the range of social science organizations on which he served in advisory or office-holding roles (see above).

In addition to this general and diffuse impact, Merton did establish several programmes that for a time shaped research in a particular area. Anomie theory in the sociology of deviance had a strong Mertonian flavour in the 1940s and 1950s, although Merton's role was solely as a theorist

Table 1 — Those referred to on at least six pages in the Index of Names in Merton (1968b)

Allport, G. W.	6	Mannheim, K.	33
Bacon, Francis	7	Marx, Karl	23
Bakke, E.	6	Mead, G. H.	9
Barber, Bernard	12	Mill, J. S.	6
Becker, Howard	9	Newcomb, T. H.	9
Bereson, Bernard	9	Newton, C.	13
Blau, Peter	6	Parsons, Talcott	30
Boyle, Robert	6	Riesman, David	6
Comte, Auguste	8	Rossi, Alice[a]	56
Cooley, Charles	8	Scheler, M.	12
Davis, Kingsley	6	Sherif, M.	6
Durkheim, Emile	31	Shils, Edward	9
Engels, Freidrich	15	Simmel, G.	19
Freud, Sigmund	14	Sorokin, Pitirim	35
Gouldner, Alvin	7	Spencer, Herbert	7
Halley, E.	6	Sprat, T.	8
Hooke, Robert	7	Stouffer, Samuel	11
Hyman, H. H.	12	Sumner, W. G.	9
Jahoda, Marie	13	Sutherland, E. H.	7
James, W.	7	Turner, R. H.	6
Katz, E.	6	Veblen, T.	10
Kendall, P. C.	6	Weber, Max	31
Laswell, H. D.	8	West, P. S.	6
Lazarsfeld, Paul[a]	50	Whitehead, A. N.	10
MacIver, R. M.	13	Znaniecki, F.	9
Malinowski, B.	9		

[a]collaborator

rather than also pursuing empirical research in this area. During the 1960s Merton developed a research programme in the sociology of science that generated much research material, and more broadly the Mertonian approach to analysing the social institution of science dominated that area of sociology. However, both these programmes soon lost their distinctiveness and became merged with broader approaches, although not without some protracted conceptual skirmishes against competing strains of analysis.

Given the empirical impetus Merton sponsored in sociology, it is appropriate that Merton's influence has been documented in a series of studies, using various forms of citation count. Several studies of authors cited in American introductory sociology texts, or in major journals, have shown Merton at least level-pegging with Parsons in textbooks through the post-World War II period: Bain (1962) for 1958–1962, Oromaner (1968) for 1963–1967, Perrucci (1980) for 1958–1977, and Wells (1979) for 1928–1976. These two authors dominate textbook citations over this period, although Wells found a slight tendency for a decline of their influence in the 1970s, and certainly found an increase in the extent to which "conflict theorists" and symbolic interactionists were cited.

The largest and most extensive of these studies (Wells and Picou, 1981, p. 110) has, *inter alia,* traced the theoretical orientations of major North American sociology journal articles using Wallace's classification (see below Chapter 4) and found that 'social structuralism' (an approach dominated by Merton) accounted for a third of work from 1936 to 1949, and approximately half thereafter. (The operationalization of Wallace's typology presents difficulties which are not addressed in this volume.)

In addition to these studies of the textbook culture and the research front of sociology, there have been studies of the citation patterns of specialist areas in sociology that throw light on his influence. A study of influential scholars in the journal literature in the sociology of race and minority group relations (Bahr *et al.,* 1971) shows that there were few citations of Merton during the 1944–56 period, but that for the 1958–1968 period he was second equal highest cited author. Of the 28 citations, 10 referenced *Social Theory and Social Structure,* rather than Merton's more specific work in this area.

A rather more sophisticated study of the sociology of science from 1950 to 1973 (Cole and Zuckerman, 1975) shows a rapid development of this specialty, and an increasing level of cognitive consensus. After a diffuse set of most-cited authors in the first half-decade studied (i.e. the early 1950s), Merton was far and away the most cited author henceforth. Cole and Zuckerman note that Merton's early work in sociology was largely ignored, and that even his return to sociology of science through as visible a forum as his 1957 Presidential Address was not marked by much citation in subsequent studies for a further decade. This lag in recognition and differential attention to the later writings is explained by a variety of factors:

— the lack of an appreciative audience, until the build-up of Sociology of Science as a specialty in the 1960s;
— resistance from historians of science whose concerns remained centred on the 'internal' cognitive development of science, rather than external social influences;

— because ". . . sociologists found in Merton's later work . . . greater 'potential for elaboration' and a reasonably clear program of research" (Cole and Zuckerman, 1975, p. 157).

Cole and Zuckerman are also able to investigate the ways in which Merton's impact was achieved:

> By and large, Merton's work is cited for two purposes: to confer authority on statements authors make and to identify the source of problems. There are few ceremonial or perfunctory citations, and [only] a few citations which are disparaging. . . . Authors who draw on Merton's work as a point of departure for their own research typically do so by developing ideas he originated or crystallized rather than using it as a source for specific hypotheses. (Zuckerman and Cole, 1975, p. 158).

A further detailed case study of the growth of scientific knowledge in the 'sociology of deviance' from 1950 to 1973 (Cole, 1975) provides further measures of Merton's impact. An extensive sample of journal articles shows Merton was the most cited author from 1955–59 through to 1965–69, with moderate attention in the half-decades before and after this period. Further study of the intellectual structure in each time period (using factor analysis of citation patterns) showed that through this 15-year period Merton's impact was largely centred within a fairly clearcut 'anomie theory' approach to devience which also included significant extensions of Merton's analysis by Cloward and Ohlin, Dubin and others. During this period, much of the remainder of the field of deviance was organised around particular types of deviance (mental illness, correctional institutions or juvenile delinquency) rather than in terms of a particular theoretical approach. By the 1970s, anomie theory no longer appears to be borne by a distinct group of writers, Merton is cited less in the major journals, and the symbolic interactionist/labelling approach arises into dominance. However, Cole notes that Merton's anomie theory continues to be widely cited outside the main journals. Of the references to Merton's work, a substantial minority is of a 'ceremonial' nature: used to support an author's approach in general terms or as part of a general literature-review, with another substantial grouping using his work to formulate a research problem or interpret data. Few attempts to empirically test Merton's ideas are reported. Cole concludes this section by suggesting that the relative decline in the more recent use of Merton's theory was because it had worked in providing a major source of puzzles, and that attention had subsequently shifted — quite irrespective of empirical groundings — to an alternative 'symbolic interactionist-labelling' approach.

Finally, Garfield (1980) has documented Merton's influences from 1970 to 1977 within sociology, amongst other social sciences, and (for 1961 to 1977) among natural sciences. A very large number of citations (2338 for the social sciences and 365 for the natural sciences) were uncovered showing a widespread influence. Most references were to *Social Theory and Social Structure*.

But these studies concentrate on statistics, rather than indicating in more depth the ways in which Merton's influence worked, so I would like to conclude this section with a small case study. The *Handbook of Medical Sociology* (Freeman *et al.*, 1972) provides a useful case study of Merton's influence in a particular area of sociology in which he had carried out some work. There are several citations of Merton's general essay on medical institutions and more intensive reporting of his work on medical education. Further, there is a scatter of references through a large number of the essays to over half-a-dozen *different* aspects of Merton's more general contributions — reference groups, anticipatory socialization and so forth. Finally, a crucial debate in a review of patient–doctor relations (Bloom and Wilson, 1972, pp. 328–330) turns on a contrast between Parsonian and Mertonian interpretations of the doctor's and the patient's roles, with the Mertonian role-set approach being held superior as it copes better with the complexities, and removes the doctor-centered approach smuggled into Parsons' definition. This case study reinforces the image of Merton's influence in sociology being definite, but diffuse.

It is unusual to be able to do more than sketch out the extent to which any one scholar has been able to influence his or her area of study. Unfortunately, these studies of Merton's impact only investigate up until the mid-1970s (except Garfield, 1980). They therefore leave unanswered the question of what the pattern of Mertonian influence has been since then. It is likely that while some specific areas of his writing continue to receive particular attention, in general the level of attention to his general theoretical work has declined. To use his own terms, much of Merton's work has been subject to "obliteration of source of ideas or findings by their incorporation in currently accepted knowledge" (1976, p. 130; see also 1968b, p. 28ff; this is abbreviated as OBI). Many of his contributions are so central that they are built into the unconsciously accepted foundations of sociology and thus have a particularly powerful intellectual influence.

Nevertheless Merton's earlier central role in having selected a stock of useful theoretical ideas has clearly been replaced by a wider variety of theoretical sources. Ben-David (1973, 1978) has made a useful point about the two-stage development of postwar American sociology that may help to indicate what the limits on Merton's *direct* influence have been. The first 'functional analysis' phase was particularly concerned with institutional description on a comparative basis. This, though, has become superseded by, or rather overlayered by, a quantitative mode of carrying out sociology. Although Merton's work may continue to have contemporary relevance it is to some considerable extent locked into the earlier phase of development in terms of its theoretical language and style of discourse. As the concerns of American sociology have changed they have increasingly limited Merton's direct impact.

However, there are signs of renewed attention to Merton's work. Of recent years much motivation to cite Merton has been to attack his stances (for example Campbell, 1982; Becker, 1984). This has the effect of raising attention to Merton's work. It is also possible, too, that Merton's writings, like those of Parsons, may participate in a revival as sociologists review the recent history of their own discipline. There seems to be widening interest from social theorists in reworking their conceptual apparatus to build in more material from not only Sociology's founding fathers but also from mid-century American social theory.

2.7   CONCLUSION

This chapter has established a framework which is a useful background for the remainder of this study. It covers Merton's biography, and especially his intellectual biography, and also the role of his work within the wider context of sociology. It is limited to published sources, and only provides a selection of the information in this; but it does begin to break new ground by establishing a periodization of Merton's work and preliminary accounts of his position in relation to sources and audiences.

3

Merton as a
discipline-builder

In charting the role Sarton played in constructing the discipline of the
history of science, Merton and Thackray (1972b) delineate several features
involved in the institutionalization of an area of study:

> The most obvious is the set of shifts that a field of learning experiences
> as it changes from being a diffuse, unfocused area of inquiry, at best
> tangential to the true intellectual concerns of its occasional votaries, to
> being a conceptually discrete discipline, able to command its own tools,
> techniques, methods, intellectual orientations and problematics. This
> creation of a cognitive identity is only one facet . . . . A set of shifts,
> which most often occurs at a later period of time, revolves around the
> creation of a professional identity for the new enterprise (p. 145).

They go on to suggest that historians of science too often concentrate on the
latter, and they also draw a distinction between the provision of the
infrastructure needed by an area of study (e.g. journals, data-banks etc.)
and the conceptual frameworks which energize it. Although Merton's own
role in relation to sociology is set within a much more complex situation, his
work has had a major impact in shaping the contemporary face of the
discipline, especially through the methodological stances he has advocated.

3.1 TOWARDS A 'SCIENTIFIC' METHODOLOGICAL STANCE
FOR SOCIOLOGY

When Merton began his professional career in the 1930s, sociology in North
America was not a strongly developed discipline. By Merton's own
account, at this time sociological thinking was dominated by concerns for

". . . the problems of urban life, family and community, of racial and ethnic groups, of poverty, crime and delinquency, and all the rest of that manifold of human problems in an industrial civilization brought into prominence by the Great Depression". (Merton, 1970a [1973, p. 173]).

Yet, on the other hand, there was also much theoretical writing in sociology which was far too general to guide more detailed sociological research and too confused with the history of social theory to combine the range of intellectual inheritances into a cumulative and compacted product. (This picture of American sociology of the 1930s is rather sharper than alternative accounts (e.g. Shils, 1970), but not substantially at variance with them.)

Merton is concerned to chart out a course that sociology might follow to extricate itself from these difficulties. Merton's detachment from grand systems of social theory was driven home dramatically by his use, as a masthead citation to *Social Theory and Social Structure,* of Whitehead's aphorism that "a science which hesitates to forget its founders is lost". The key image he puts forward is of sociology as an advancing, accumulative science generally based on a 'natural science' model and sharply demarcated from 'common-sense' social knowledge. This is to be achieved mainly through theoretical activity, working up new theories and consolidating smaller-scope theories into wider theoretical structures. But the theories are to be of a particular type, theories of the middle-range located between broad-scale theoretical orientations on the one hand and small-scale empirical generalizations on the other. The conceptual device of 'paradigms' is advanced to encourage the systematic consolidation of areas of study (1949b [1968b]).

This theme of the cumulation of sociology through middle-range theory is constantly repeated in many of Merton's essays, as well as being centrally located as a main theme of his *Social Theory and Social Structure.* The foundation of this stance was laid in the introduction to the first edition of this book, together with the pair of short essays, written at about the same time, that deal with each side of the interplay between theory and research ("The bearing of sociological theory on empirical research" and "The bearing of empirical research on sociological theory": 1945c, and 1948b).

Merton's subsequent writing only slightly extended or modified the methodological stance laid out in the mid- and late 1940s. This basic doctrine was, however, extended in his essays on applied sociology (1949c, 1963b), formalization of theory (1954), the relationship between sociology and psychology (1957a), problem-selection (1959a), the anti-sociologist's canon (1961b), the role of the sociologist in relation to social problems (1976a) , the role of theory classics (1967a), the role of values in social science (1971) and the conception of 'theoretical pluralism' (1975a, 1981a).

(It is possible that this set of methodological points adds up to an overall methodological stance, but this question is not explored here. It also should be noted that Merton has drawn attention to methodological concerns in a wide variety of his writings — for example 1943b, 1957a, 1977.)

Merton's methodological stance was later modified in two significant aspects. His sharp demarcation between the history of sociology and its presently advancing research front is relaxed in a 1967 essay on the "History and Systematics of Social Theory" (1968b) which brings his 'methodological ideology' into line with his own practice by enumerating the useful ways in which the classical tradition can feed into contemporary sociology. He also points up that this contact with the legacy of social thought stresses the 'humanistic' aspects of Sociology.

In several essays on conflicting and competing approaches in sociology, (1961b,1972a) Merton relaxes his unitary image of sociology to point up a conception of sociology as a multi-paradigm or theoretically pluralist science, in which theories derived from different theoretical approaches can shed complementary, rather than incommensurate, insights into social phenomena.

Merton's methodological stance carried weight not so much because it was original but because of its careful, detailed and well-written presentation. Certainly, it is far less crude than some alternative contemporary images, such as Lundberg's social physics, and more concrete than many other stances. Nor am I arguing that his published methodological stance had a 'causal' impact, such that its exposition alone had a strong impact in setting sociology on its scientific feet. Rather, his methodological doctrine suited an emerging climate of opinion in sociology and helped to shape and justify this. But this is no mean achievement, as some of the praise for the successful development of American sociology in the post-war period can be given to Merton's methodological writings, together with some of the blame for the deficiencies of the empiricism (the doctrine that theory unproblematically flows from social facts) that it unintentionally seemed to support.

Merton was instrumental, not only in helping to build a cumulative sociology from its earlier 'social problems' and 'history of ideas' components, but also in building into the core of this cumulative sociological enterprise various emerging components (such as social survey research). So Merton both distanced his vision of sociology from earlier work and also knitted together newer aspects into a workable coalition of interests.

As might be expected, this attempt to stitch together the methodological frameworks necessary for a cumulating sociology did not nicely and neatly flow from the published doctrine, but was rather more complex. The doctrines themselves had unintended consequences, and took sociology into directions not contemplated.

One outcome of his work was the development of a 'theory-construction school' within sociology which stressed the importance of the more formal statement of theories. Central to this enterprise was Merton's startling formalized casting of Durkheim's theory of suicide:

1. Social cohesion provides psychic support to group members subjected to acute stresses and anxieties. 2. Suicide rates are functions of unrelieved anxieties and stresses to which persons are subjected. 3. Catholics have greater cohesion than Protestants. 4. Therefore, lower suicide rates should be anticipated among Catholics than among Protestants. (1948b [1968b, p. 151])

The development of the 'theory-building school' began in the early 1950s with Zetterberg (1965 [1954]) and flourished into the early 1970s. A signal concern in the dozen or so theory-construction texts which were written over this period was the continued development of Merton's formalization of Durkheim's theory of suicide. While this 'school' may have helped clarify sociological thinking about the nature of formal theories, there was also a tendency to value the 'formal means' of theorizing over the 'content' of the theories and thus too often these books became bogged down in technicalities.

3.2   MERTON'S IMAGE OF SCIENCE

Merton draws on the cognitive authority accorded natural science to bolster his methodological views. His image of science is fairly straightforward and unexamined. He portrays the need for huge inputs of person power over extended periods, the need for careful accumulation of empirical studies which extend and develop lines of investigation, the necessity of a modest stance which stresses the tentativeness of scientific statements and the requirement of an aloofness from both the common-sense of public views and the demands for immediate application and relevance. Above the dull patient mass of scientific workers there is a role for scientific geniuses (Newton, Einstein, etc.), but Merton makes it clear that he sees their role as one of consolidation of an accumulation of findings into pithy summative perspectives, rather than that of revolutionary thinkers opening up cognitive realms for the regiment of empirical research workers to invade. The image corresponds to Kuhn's image of the 'normal' phase of science, without any hint of any revolutionary irruptions to an essentially linear growth of progress over the long-run. Merton is, however, very sensitive to discontinuities and change over the short-run (1965, 1967a). The role of empirical research is seen very largely to extend a research programme rather than to carry out any strategic tests to overthrow it.

Merton sees little need to differentiate social science from this vision of scientific progress, apart from the crucial difference with which he flays social scientists — the need for due modesty in the face of the scientific youthfulness of the social sciences. He pessimistically draws the analogy that "Perhaps sociology is not yet ready for its Einstein because it has not yet found its Kepler — to say nothing of its Newton, Laplace, Gibbs, Maxwell or Planck" (1968b, p. 47). Just because sociology coexists at the same time as the natural sciences does not mean that it has a similar degree of maturity. His later doctrine (1968b [1967a]) is rather more sensitive to differences between the natural and social sciences, but nevertheless these differences are still seen to lie in the historical stage of development of the discipline rather than in features inherent in social phenomena. This means that the social sciences must adopt a mix of historical erudition and contemporary intellectual enterprise in their approaches to study. There has been some criticism of the extent to which this 'natural science' model has been imported into Merton's methodological writings in relation to sociology : for example, Baldamus (1976) has criticized the use of the term 'discovery' to also apply to the social science sphere. Perhaps an insufficient discrimination between the domains of natural and social science is a cost that must be set alongside the advantages of the many careful lessons Merton has been able to draw from his study of natural science and natural scientists.

The image of science is presented without any fanfare. No particular appeal to the writings or behaviour of scientists is made, nor is his doctrine backed by citing philosophers of science. (Later, he does claim assent to this policy from Plato, Bacon, John Stuart Mill and George Cornewall Lewis [1968b, pp. 56–64] and also a number of contemporary writers: especially T. H. Marshall.) Yet, his account of science is rather more plausible and complex than other doctrines circulating at the time (for example, Lundberg's ideal of a 'social physics') and it must be remembered that by the mid-1940s there was little readily available useful writing in the philosophy of science to be drawn upon. Indeed, when discussing the implications of the multi-paradigm/plural theory situation of sociology Merton extensively draws on the philosophical literature which reacted to Kuhn's image of science (1976a).

To some sociologists, Merton might well appear to be a 'positivist' or even an 'empiricist'. Indeed, Merton would seem to accept at least to a considerable degree the various assumptions that positivists are considered to cleave to (cf. Wilson, 1983, pp. 11–17). However, his positivism is always of a 'weak' and sophisticated variety which stresses the centrality of theoretical work. Moreover, Merton has recorded his distaste for cruder versions of these doctrines he was exposed to in his early years as a scholar (1934, 1985).

3.3   THE DOCTRINE OF MIDDLE-RANGE THEORY

The central methodological precept for which Merton is undoubtedly most famous is his advocacy of 'theories of the middle-range'. This directly addresses the two deficiencies Merton had identifed in then-contemporary sociology, and suggests avoiding the pitfalls of either by driving in between. It is important, then, to clearly present his stance on this point. The key passage was indicated in an address in 1947 and published in 1949 (1968b, p. 39):

> Middle-range theory is principally used in sociology to guide empirical inquiry. It is intermediate to general theories of social systems which are too remote from particular classes of social behaviour, organization and change to account for what is observed and to those detailed orderly descriptions of particulars that are not generalized at all. Middle-range theory involves abstractions, of course, but they are close enough to observed data to be incorporated in propositions that permit empirical testing. Middle-range theories deal with delimited aspects of social phenomena, as is indicated by their labels. One speaks of a theory of reference groups, of social mobility, or role-conflict and of the formation of social norms just as one speaks of a theory of prices, a germ theory of disease, or a kinetic theory of gases.

Middle-range theories are distinguished from general sociological orientations ("Such orientations involve broad postulates which indicate types of variables which are somehow to be taken into account" — 1968b, pp. 41, 42) and empirical generalizations ("an isolated proposition summarising observed uniformities of relationships between two or more variables" — 1968b, p. 149).

Some of the characteristics of middle-range theory noted are:

— the seminal ideas in such theories are characteristically simple (1968b, p. 40).
— the idea itself is tested for its fruitfulness by noting the range of

theoretical problems and hypotheses that allow one to identify new characteristics of . . . [the phenomenon pointed up by the imagery of the theory] (1968b, p. 40).

— [it is not just an image for thinking about an aspect of a phenomenon, but it] generate[s] distinctive problems for sociological inquiry . . . [and] . . . points directly to relevant empirical research (1968b, pp. 42, 43).

— [it provides understanding of a phenomenon by, for example] . . . identifying the social mechanisms [which generate it, and then] . . . discovering how those mechanisms came into being, so that we can explain why the mechanisms do not operate effectively or fail to emerge at all in some social systems (1968b, pp. 42, 43).

— they are frequently consistent with a variety of so-called systems of sociological theory (1968b, p. 43).

— these theories do not remain separate but are consolidated into wider networks of theory (1968b, p. 68).

— this type of theory cuts across the distinction between microsociological problems . . . and macrosociological problems (1968b, p. 68).

The examples he gives are: the theories of social mobility, reference groups, relative deprivation, social stratification, authority, change, institutional interdependence, anomie, role conflict, and formation of social norms (1968b, pp. 40,41), dissonance and social differentiation (1968b, p. 64) and theories of racial, class and international conflict (1968b, p. 68). (This listing is a significant pointer to those areas of his work that Merton considers theoretically significant, and this will be picked up in Chapters 4 and 5.)

The middle-range approach was aggressively deployed as an alternative to Parsons's proposal that sociology should concentrate on developing general theory. Drawing on his general image of how scientific knowledge advances Merton considered this call premature, and hence doomed to failure. The explication of the middle-range approach was a useful outcome of the debate. Nevertheless, Merton closed his extended debate with Parsons over the most appropriate theory-building strategy on a conciliatory note (or more precisely, footnote) in the third edition of *Social Theory and Social Structure* (1968b, p. 52) in which Merton stresses that their differences lay only over the most appropriate means for gaining the same scientific end.

A key characteristic of middle-range theories is that they should cut across different institutional areas of sociological investigation, and that they apply across different historical societies. As Kolb (1958) suggests in reviewing the second edition of *Social Theory and Social Structure* "'Middle-range theory', then, must mean not a middle level of abstraction but rather theory at the highest level of abstraction in dealing with social systems but concerned only with selected aspects of those systems" (p. 545).

In practice there has been a slewing away from this doctrine (for example, see Willer, 1967, pp. xii–xvi, Alexander, 1982, pp. 11–15). It is often taken as a justification for merely tacking a few explicit theorems onto the beginning of the presentation of an empirical study. In the apparent absence of exercises which sweep up a range of middle-order theories into consolidated wider frameworks, it is possible that, in practice, this doctrine has not assisted in the cumulation of sociological knowledge. If the achievements from this doctrine have not met the standards it attempted to set, nevertheless, it did provoke much more attention to theory in the everyday practice of sociology.

A difficulty with the middle-range theory strategy lies in the art of couching theories at the exact pitch of abstractness and degree of empirical connectedness. Few can pitch social theory in a way that captures essentially human features of the operation of social structures while avoiding too much historical specificity or retention of the particular flavour of some institutional area. It is not entirely accidental that almost all the examples Merton uses (apart from those drawn from the natural sciences) are his own. The right mix of abstractness is often more easily developed in work with small groups, or perhaps formal organizations, and so it is not surprising that many of Merton's middle-range theories have been developed in his micro-sociology.

3.4   OTHER ASPECTS OF MERTON'S METHODOLOGY

Merton's doctrine of 'middle-range' theory is embedded in a broader framework stressing the importance to sociology of developing testable theories of empirical data.

Much of the methodological impact of Merton's image of a scientific sociology was carried by the pair of essays (1945c, 1948b [1968b]) which examine the bearing of social theory on research and of social research on theory. The first essay differentiates several conceptions of theory, especially contrasting theory proper with general sociological orientations on the one hand and empirical generalizations and ad hoc explanations on the other.

In the second essay of the pair, research is seen as initiating, reformulating, deflecting and clarifying theory. In particular, Merton urges alertness to the possibility of 'serendipity': the unanticipated discovery of theoretically strategic facts. How this image of dynamic and complex interplay can be dismissed by Dahrendorf (1968, p. 120) as "very mechanical" is difficult to understand.

Merton is concerned that 'proper' (that is, middle-range) sociological theories should be 'explanatory' in form. Usually, this is taken to require specifying alternative behavioural outcomes which are specifically linked to particular different social structural situations. For example, in commenting on Cloward's extension to anomie theory, Merton (1959b) reproves him for providing no more than a typological exercise, however fruitful he considers the suggested extended typology to be.

This concern with locating the grain of social reality, so that its structure can be revealed through a clean, deep conceptual axe-cut, had the consequence of deflecting attention from philosophical issues about the nature of social reality. Perhaps a further consequence has been the inability of Merton's theorizing to cope with the recent growth of Continental social thought with its often more heavily-scored philosophical concerns.

However, Merton recognizes a role for general social theory in providing basic imagery from which more specific theories can be generated (1968b, pp 141–143). For example, he suggests that: " . . . to the extent that the general thoeretical orientation provided by Marxism becomes a guide to systematic empirical research, it must do so by developing intermediate special [i.e. middle-range] theories" (1968b, p. 66). In cultivating the development of such theories Merton enumerates several functions of classical social theoretical writings: "These range from the direct pleasure of coming upon an aesthetically pleasing and more cogent version of one's own ideas, through the satisfaction of independent confirmation of these ideas by a powerful mind, and the educative function of developing high standards of taste for sociological work to the interactive effect of developing new ideas by turning to older writings within the context of contemporary knowledge" (1968b, p. 37). He also spells out an active process of codifying (1968b, p. 155) in which the abstract qualities of theories are encouraged by progressively stripping lower-order theories of their empirical limitations.

Much of the appeal in Merton's sociology lies in its working within and against common-sense. Merton utilized the dramatic potential in sociology for taking the common-sense stance and then sharply circumscribing its limits and exposing the unexpected 'rationality' of the opposite viewpoint. In several widely circulated pieces Merton related sociology to common-sense (see 3.6 below).

3.5   PARADIGMS AS A METHODOLOGICAL DEVICE

One methodological tool used by Merton to assist in codifying areas of study is a what he terms a qualitative paradigm. That these are considered central tools in his vision of the progress of sociology is attested by Merton's several references to them (1948c [1968b, pp. 69—72, 104—109] and 1976b, pp. 209—216). As examples, he lists his paradigms for functional analysis in sociology and the sociology of knowledge, and as worked examples ("delimited paradigms") those relating to anomie, intermarriage and prejudice-discrimination.

Paradigms are seen as not just notational devices, but as 'logical designs for analysis' which ". . . bring out into the open the array of assumptions, concepts and basic propositions employed in a sociological investigation" (1976b, p. 211) and also as ". . . preliminary efforts to assemble propositional inventions of sociological knowledge" (1976b, p. 211). They are seen as having five related functions:

— notational (by setting out concepts in a summary form);
— avoidance of inadvertent oversight (by providing a check-list of concepts);
— enhancement of accumulation (by providing a framework allowing extra theoretical interpretations to be added);
— promotion of the cross-tabulation of concepts;
— enhancing codification by providing a framework for assembling qualitative information.

The methodological role of paradigms in Merton's sense has some distant similarity to Max Weber's tool of 'ideal types', and is unfortunately afflicted with a similar ambiguity. But Merton's device, unlike Weber's, has fortunately not generated a confusing and unproductive secondary literature. This is largely because the term was effectively kidnapped by Kuhn (1962), and used rather differently as a tool to refer to the set of ideas and research practices shared by research communities.

In my interpretation, Merton's conception spans at least four types:

— the paradigm of functional analysis involves a listing of steps to be undertaken and issues to be confronted in carrying out a functional analysis;
— the paradigm of the sociology of knowledge sketches out a conceptual framework of the types of variables and the relationships between them, that allows alternative theories about particular linkages to be mapped out;

— the paradigms of anomie and prejudice-discrimination are typologies of 'modes of adaptation' or 'behavioural patterns';
— a paradigm is seen as providing a framework, analogous to statistical handling of quantitative data, for analysing qualitative data (but no example is given of this).

Of these types, the third is more appropriately termed a typology. As such it can be found (see Chapter 5 below) to be endemic to Merton's implicit theoretical model and thus more widely used in his own writings than Merton might suggest. The multi-purpose character of a paradigm is surely being stretched too far by trying to enlist it as a framework in actual research studies, as in the fourth usage. (Indeed Lazarsfeld's concept of an 'accounting scheme'(1975, pp. 45–56) might be more appropriate here.)

The first and second usages blend together more if the methodological function of the first is downplayed and its review function emphasized. It is the second usage that is most important. Laying out the major conceptual units in a field of study is a useful approach to building up codifications of both theories and research findings in a problem-area. The time at which the device was first proposed underlines the value of this more formal approach even more.

As Merton himself notes, more explicit and direct theories can be developed if the prevalent discursive essay format of the sociology of the time could be broken up into more graspable and workable argument-structures in which the exact formulations of the theories are exposed. Merton, although himself a master of the essay form, is trying to validate a different style of discourse. This is emphasized in the awkward analogy he draws between paradigms and data analysis procedures for quantitative variables. A more recent term used to describe a similar type of analytically reviewing of a field is 'meta-analysis'.

Interestingly, the paradigm (analytical framework) is not seen by Merton as a device for cumulating general theory from an aggregation of middle-range theories. And yet surely this is a function of a paradigm, and could easily be developed to complement the doctrine of 'middle-range' theorizing. One of the tasks of a general theory is to provide the framework for setting up the paradigm within which alternative middle-range theories can nest. Developing the notion of paradigm in this direction has another payoff as it allows us to glimpse the essential commonality between the Mertonian and the Kuhnian versions of the concept: paradoxically, Merton gives the term a 'normative' usage to suggest what a cognitive framework in an area ought to be, whereas Kuhn uses the concept 'sociologically' to indicate what the conceptual structure in an area actually is.

3.6 OTHER MODES OF INFLUENCE

Undoubtedly, Merton's main influence in the discipline-rebuilding of sociology lay through his methodological writing. But in addition, there are several other aspects of his theoretical work which served to bring together some of the multifarious strands of post-World War II American sociology. It is through these mechanisms, according to my analysis, that Merton played his role in helping to shape the central directions of sociology.

Merton's laying out of a common mainstream methodological position to which most sociologists could actively adhere was flanked with an active public defence of sociology (e.g. "The Canons of the Anti-Sociologist" (1961b [1973]). As a public defender of sociology, Merton had some advantages over Parsons whose heavy prose induced respect for its theoretical sophistication but opprobrium for its density. Several of Merton's formulations 'in support for sociology' were popular — for example, Merton's insistence that:

> the distinctive intellectual contributions of the sociologist are found primarily in the study of unintended consequences (among which are latent functions) of social practises,as well as in the study of anticipated consequences (among which are manifest functions). (1949b [1968b, p. 120])

Another useful point was his neat contrast of the banner of (European) sociologists of knowledge "We don't know that what we say is true, but it is at least significant" with the (American) empirical researchers' claim that "We don't know that what we say is particularly significant, but it is at least true" (1968b, p. 494).

Alongside his explicit methodological positions Merton's theoretical stances were sympathetic, and therefore attractive, to the development of empirical sociology. Most of Merton's work was carried out with a close connection to possible or actual empirical research investigations. This helped to link with a wide range of empirical researchers. For example, in two crisp sentences Merton nicely linked survey research into his theoretical concerns:

> The categories of audience measurement have been primarily those of income stratification (a kind of datum obviously important to those ultimately concerned with selling and marketing their commodities), sex, age and education (obviously important for those seeking to learn the advertising outlets most appropriate for reaching special groups). But since such categories as sex, age, education and income happen also

to correspond to some of the chief statuses in the social structure, the procedures evolved for audience measurement by the students of mass communication are of direct interest to the sociologist as well (1949b [1968b, p. 505]).

Although Merton has been largely concerned with developing his own theoretical analyses, he also often played a role in showing how different theories can complement each other. In a comparison of four alternative theories of deviance, Merton (1976a, pp.31–37) shows how each highlights a particular area of phenomena while leaving other aspects in darkness. While some theories can be combined, others clash or give rise to competing hypotheses and others 'talk past each other' (see Fig. 2).

THEORY	PROBLEM	IGNORES
differential association	cultural transmission of deviance	original development
anomie–and–opportu-nity structures	structural sources	cultural transmission
labelling theory/societal reaction	formation of deviant careers	subsequent careers
conflict theory	formation of legal rules	differing rates

Fig. 2 — Relationship between different theories of deviance.

Finally, Merton was better able to influence the development of his approach to sociology because he was strategically located for putting it into effect through teaching and books. Merton was able to influence the training in social theory of a significant group of several generations of American sociologists, since over this period Columbia continued to attract large cohorts of graduate students who were subsequently successful in sociological careers. The effectiveness of this education was considerably enhanced by the education in methods fostered by Lazarsfeld, and especially by the joint effect of both Merton and Lazarsfeld and the interplay between them.

An important way in which the ideas of a 'school' are disseminated is through publications. We have already noted Merton's role in organizing two important published symposia (a general review of the state of the art in sociology and another on sociology and social problems). While Merton did not himself write any textbooks, he played an active role in shaping several exemplary introductory textbooks — Kingsley Davis's (1948) *Human Society,* Johnson's (1960) *Sociology,* and more recently Cole's (1972; 2nd edn 1979) *The Sociological Orientation.* More generally, Merton was able to place something of his stamp, through close editing and advice, on a wider set of influential texts that constitute a veritable sociological library: including a set of sociological readings (Coser and Rosenberg, 1959; 2nd edn 1964), a history of social thought (Coser, 1977 [1971]) and a social research methodology text (Riley, 1963).

As has already been indicated, *Social Theory and Social Structure* served in its overall effect as an exemplar. Beyond this, Merton played an important role in organizing and carefully editing two significant discipline-wide surveys in the late 1960s and early 1970s. *Sociology Today* was based on sessions organized for the 1957 ASA meetings and attempted to review the 'problematics' of some thirty fields of sociology.

Contemporary Social Problems was a definite attempt to sum up the contemporary sociological knowledge that addressed the social problems of the time. A characteristically wide, if not radical, net was cast in constructing this book, including attention to social class as a source of social problems. Again, although not locked into formal organizational roles, Merton was also involved in activities aimed at extending the continuing internationalization of sociology by giving key addresses on the social role of sociology and the sociology of its internal divisions.

But as well as helping to shape the 'form' of postwar sociology, Merton had a considerable influence on its 'content', and it is to an elucidation of this that this study now turns.

4

Merton's general theory I: manifest theoretical stance

4.1 INTRODUCTION: DEFINITION OF SOCIOLOGY

It is doubtful whether Merton could have played such a central role in shaping the methodological direction of sociology (as described in Chapter 3), without the intellectual authority he was also able to achieve through his substantive contributions to the discipline. In turn, his highly visible substantive contributions helped to make concrete and to validate his discipline-building role. Each role complemented and reinforced the other.

In this chapter, Merton's own depiction of his theoretical programme is sketched out. This is followed in the next chapter by a reconstruction of the several elements that can be seen to be implicitly involved in his general approach. Through this double consideration, at both manifest and latent levels, I will attempt to show the analytical base on which Merton's reputation as a theorist has been built. A subsequent chapter will then show how this general model is involved in Merton's substantive analyses.

It is difficult to find a clear and straightforward definition of sociology within Merton's writing. (This is perhaps characteristic given his lack of attention to such housekeeping details.) However, while addressing a wider audience in his "The Canons of the Anti-Sociologist" (1976b, p. 184) he suggests that: "In the large, sociology is engaged in finding out how man's behaviour and fate are affected, if not minutely governed, by his place within particular kinds, and changing kinds, of social structure and of culture". At another point, sociology is referred to as the science of the group (1968b, p. 363). At yet another point, Merton has provided a short listing of characteristic questions raised by sociologists (1957a, p. 56):

— How is social organization to be conceived, what are its principal attributes, and how are these connected?
— Which properties and structures of social organization enable indivi-

duals to operate with greater or less effectiveness within their social setting?

— What processes in a social organization foster or curb the achievement of the goals of individuals within them, enabling these to be realized with greater or less stress?

— What are the regularities in the sequences of social status to be assumed by individuals within the organization or society? what are the effects of discontinuities and continuities in these sequences of status?

— The culture of society incorporates the values men in that society live by. How does the structure of the society facilitate or hamper the efforts of men, variously located in that structure, to act in terms of these cultural values?

4.2   MERTON AS A FUNCTIONAL ANALYST

Merton has somewhat studiously avoided too explicit a theoretical stance within the broad parameters set by the 'middle-range' approach discussed in the previous chapter. However, in *Social Theory and Social Structure* (1968b) he explicitly stakes a claim to being a 'functional analyst' and this is claimed in the Introduction to the first and second editions (1957a, p. 3) to be the framework which ties together the remainder of the book (the third edition does not include a general introduction as several passages in it are expanded into full-scale essays in their own right).

The Preface to the third edition does not attempt to provide a definition, let alone a programmatic statement of this position. Instead the reader is directed to Chapter 3, in which a paradigm for functional analysis is laid out. Here we do find a definition: "the practice of interpreting data by establishing their consequences for the larger structures in which they are implicated" (1968b, p. 101).

In his essay, Merton is concerned to elucidate the key points of functional analysis as a mode of sociological interpretation. To emphasize the logic of functional analysis Merton strips down the theoretical content involved. In some contrast, Parsons's 'structural-functional' analysis was developed as a general theory of how social integration was accomplished (through a basic consensus over values and norms and other social machinery) and had negligible stress on the methodology involved. The key features of Mertonian functional analysis are that it sees social systems as collections of parts, and is concerned to analyse the complex relationships of interdependence among these parts. Functionalism was originally an approach fashioned by anthropologists to analyse regularities behind the cultural complexities of nonliterate societies, rather than for tracing the evolution of cultural forms. Merton is able to take this, and to convert it to an approach suited to the analysis of modern societies. He is concerned to take anthropological conceptual equipment and turn it to sociological use.

Merton begins his essay with some terminological notes setting out alternative usages of the term, with a concern to establish a technical definition. Following this definitional exercise, a formal programme (described as a 'paradigm') is laid out of the agenda of methodological issues that functional analyses must address (or it might be construed, the steps through which a functional analysis might advance: 1949b [1968b, pp. 104–108]). This involves (in my reworked presentation):

(1) identification and description of the item (social or cultural phenomenon) to be analysed;

(2) analysis of the motivation (or motives, purposes or subjective dispositions) of the individuals involved;

(3) identification and description of the system within which the item is set;

(4) analysis of the objective consequences of the item, especially for the system;

(5) separation of the schedule of objective consequences into 'functions' (". . . those observed consequences which make for the adaptation or adjustment of a given system . . .") 'dysfunctions' (". . . which lessen the adaptation or adjustment of the system"), and 'nonfunctions' (which are functionally irrelevant) and a 'net balance of the aggregate of consequences';

(6) separation of objective consequences (in relation to the previous analysis of motives) into those which are manifest functions (". . . intended and recognized by participants . . .") and those which are latent functions ("neither intended nor recognized");

(7) analysis of the 'functional requirements' (or needs or prerequisites) of the system;

(8) identification and description of the (social) mechanisms through which functions are fulfilled;

(9) analysis of functional alternatives (equivalents or substitutes) by specifying the range of possible variation amongst the items in the system capable of subserving a functional requirement;

(10) analysis of the structural context or structural constraint on the range of variation in the items which can effectively satisfy functional requirements (especially, analysis of the interrelationships which lock items into the system and ensure that their elimination would affect the rest of the system);

(11) attention to the functional analysis of dynamics and change;
(12) attention to the development of approaches to validate functional analyses (especially through comparative or quasi-experimental research designs);
(13) attention to the ideological implications of functional analyses.

I think that this listing can be usefully grouped into three areas:

— steps involved with carrying out a partial functional analysis (steps (1) to (6)) in which an item is analysed in relation to its context (but the context is not necessarily seen as a 'system');
— steps involved with carrying out a full systemic functional analysis of a system (steps (7) to (10));
— points of wider methodological concern to functional analyses generally (steps (11) to (13)).

Merton points up the major methodological difficulties standing in the way of carrying out a full systemic functional analysis. He suggests that the idea of functional requisites "remains one of the cloudiest and empirically most debatable concepts in functional theory" and that ". . . as utilized by sociologists the concept of functional requisites tends to be tautological or even ex post facto" (1968b, p. 106).

In his portrayal of functional analysis Merton develops several points. He is at some pains to distance his version from the 'classical' mode of functional analysis as developed in anthropological writings of the 1920s and 1930s. (However, several commentators have suggested that Merton's reconstruction of classical functional analysis is 'forced': e.g. Davis, 1959). To adapt functional analysis to the study of more complex societies is seen to require a rejection of three postulates usually held to be 'essential' to classical functional analysis (1968b, pp. 79–91):

— the postulate of the functional unity of society (that is, that ". . . every culturally standardized activity or belief is functional for the society as a whole and uniformly functional for [all] the people living in it" :1968b, p. 81);
— the postulate of universal functionalism (which ". . . holds that all standardized social or cultural forms have positive functions": 1968b, p. 84);
— the postulate of indispensability (that "there are certain functions which are indispensable in the sense that, unless they are performed, the society (or group or individual) will not persist . . [and] . . that certain

cultural or social forms are indispensable for fulfilling each of these functions": 1968b, p. 87).

This rejection of the trinity of classical functional postulates has several direct implications for a reformulated functional analysis: that the consequences of social units for other areas of social life be recognized as: multiple, specified as either functional or dysfunctional, and not inherently tied to a particular form (but rather, units may have alternatives).

Another concern in his essay is his detailed rebuttal of the logical necessity of the conservative ideological freight often thought to be carried by functional analysis: by skilfully comparing ideological orientations shared by dialectical materialism and functional analysis Merton is able to claim that a radical impulse (as well as the admitted usual conservative patina) can be associated with functional analysis, and is able to conclude that ". . . functional analysis may involve no intrinsic ideological commitment . . ." (Merton, 1968b, p. 93). This early formulation of the functional principles underlying several forms of Marxism has later been taken up by more recent commentators.

Some attention in this essay is also devoted to laying out the descriptive material required in any research study (1968b, pp. 109–114), including:

— a description, in social structural terms, of participation in the observed pattern;
— an indication of the principal alternatives to the observed pattern which are excluded (i.e. the boundaries of the pattern, especially in comparison with those pertaining crossculturally);
— the meanings of the pattern to the actors;
— the array of motives associated with the pattern;
— those regularities of behaviour associated with the pattern, but not recognized by participants, as part of the pattern.

But perhaps the leading methodological argument in this crucial essay on functional analysis concerns the 'heuristic purposes' of the identification of latent functions (i.e. those not intended or recognized by participants: see above) for theoretical work in sociology. Merton argues that identification of latent functions (1968b, pp. 118-126):

— "clarifies the analysis of seemingly irrational social patterns" (that may serve wide social functions while not achieving their ostensible purposes, especially in terms of Western physical science);
— "directs attention to theoretically fruitful fields of inquiry" (by by-

passing the rather more obvious and restricted questions posed by only examining manifest functions);
— ". . . represents significant increments in sociological knowledge" (because the uncovering of latent functions represents greater departures from 'commonsense' knowledge, by exposing an added level of complexity in social life);
— "precludes the substitution of naive moral judgements for sociological analysis" (as moral judgements often only encompass manifest consequences);
— "by imply[ing] the concept of strain, stress and tension on the structural level, provides an analytical approach to the study of dynamics and change" (1968b, p. 107).

Merton's discussion of functional analysis is larded with a wide range of examples — religion in modern sociology, magic, the Chiricahua puberty ceremonial for girls, patterned responses to mirriri (hearing obscenity directed at one's sister), the 'romantic love complex' in American society, the cultural pattern of conspicuous consumption, taboo on out-marriage, hostility to deviants, Polish peasant cooperative institutions, Hopi rainfall ceremonies, the effect of the researcher in the Hawthorne studies, and the North American 'political machine'. Most are briefly referred to, but the functions of religion, the pattern of conspicuous consumption and especially the role of the political machine are addressed at greater length. This analysis of the political machine has been recognised as a particularly important contribution apart from its usefulness as an illustration (Landau, 1968).

A summary of this example may be useful in providing a more concrete specification of how Merton saw, at that stage in his writing, what was involved in carrying out a functional analysis (in my paraphrase):

American political machines were generally considered to be evils, allowed to continue only because of 'deficiencies' in the running of American local government, especially because of the insufficient exercise of political strength by 'responsible citizens' to secure reform. However, attention to latent functions points to other deficiences in official local government structures which make it difficult for effective decisions and action to take place so that they do not seem to serve the 'human' needs and expectations of their 'clientele'. The political machine fulfils these needs of ordinary men and women more effectively, by providing aid suited to the diverse needs of different groups, in a manner that does not stigmatize its recipients. For those in groups that find it difficult to achieve upward mobility, in a society renowned for its cultural emphasis on 'getting ahead', the machine offers alternative channels of social mobility. For business people, political machines expedite business efficiency by cutting through the red tape which surrounds the divided bureaucracies. For 'illegitimate business' (crime) engaged, as is legitimate business, in the provision of goods and services for which there is an economic demand, the political machine provides 'protection' from undue government interference and a rationalization of the organization of the services. The deep-rooted needs that the structure (i.e. the political machine) fulfils means that it will be difficult to eradicate without complex social engineering. Merton completes his analysis by pointing out that the structure may come to quite transparently show up the functions, as when the social opposites — but functional similars — of the big businessman and the big racketeer both meet " . . . in the smoke-filled room of the successful politician" (see 1968b, p. 135).

4.3   COMMENTARY ON MERTON'S FUNCTIONAL ANALYSIS

Having provided a fairly extensive summary of Merton's account of functional analysis, I will now provide a brief commentary that seeks to elicit some of the more salient points about this presentation. This commentary begins with a few points of a general and terminological nature and then pursues a more detailed critique. It continues with some notes on some rather different questions: about the extent to which Merton actually uses a functional mode of analysis, and the social context of its development.

(1) Why does Merton use the term 'functional analysis' rather than the more full-blooded 'structural-functionalism' sported by Talcott Parsons? Parsons himself (1975, p. 67) reports that in a meeting in 1961:

Merton very cogently made the point of objecting to the phrase 'structural-functionalism'. He particularly did not like having it labelled as an 'ism' and suggested that the simple descriptive phrase 'functional analysis' was more 'appropriate'.

(Parsons appears not to have noted Merton's usage in *Social Theory and Social Structure* since Merton had been using the term since 1949 at least.) Presumably the suffix 'ism' was deprecated because of its connotation that it involved a whole social movement or canon of principles. Merton was clearly not particularly concerned to use a slightly different label to signal any substantive difference from Parsons's theoretical approach (as opposed to his explicit distancing of himself from Parsons's 'grand theory' theory-building style as has been described in Chapter 3).

(2) What theoretical freight does 'functional analysis' carry? Mertonian functional analysis is not strongly linked to any other particular theoretical programme in sociology: it does not carry with it much in the way of additional theoretical assumptions, such as the 'value-consensus' ideas in Parsonian thought. Certainly, one of the 'virtues' of Mertonian functional analysis is its eclectic span; little is required in the way of specific units or approaches to defining social phenomena. Witness the listing of items to which functions might be imputed (1968b, p. 104):

> social roles, institutional patterns, social processes, cultural pattern, culturally patterned emotions, social norms, group organization, social structure, devices for social control etc. [and the listing of the types of unit for which an item might have consequences] . . . individuals in diverse statuses, subgroups, the large social system and culture systems (1968b, p. 106).

(3) Does functional analysis supply explanations? Wallace complains that ". . . Merton and Davis refer somewhat indiscriminantly to functional 'analysis', 'theory', 'method' and still more vaguely to 'an interpretational schema [that] depends upon a triple alliance between theory, method and data' . . " :1969, p. 25). However, Merton does separate out causal from functional analyses, particularly in his definition of functional analysis and in his examination of the political machine, although this has been over-looked by most commentators. His definition uses the limited term 'inter-pretation'. Merton's main example explicitly contrasts (1949c [1968b, p. 125]) the causal explanations of the rise and continuance of political machines (in terms of the lack of political efficacy by the 'respectable' who are not able to reform the machines) with 'supplementary' functional interpretations (which show that it is in the interests of a variety of client groups that political machines should continue).

(4) Does Merton use both partial and full functional analyses? Only part of the thirteen-point conceptual armoury of functional analysis is deployed in any detail in the essay, and especially the main example. No examples of full systemic-type functional analyses are given (as several commentators, e.g. Mulkay (1971), have noted). Amongst the partial functional analyses provided, it is ironic that dysfunctions are not analysed (as Cuzzort (1969) has also pointed out; although it seems to me that analysing the dysfunc-

tions of a 'deviant structure' involves some similarity in stance to the analysing of the [eu]functions of their 'legitimate' structural alternatives).

(5) How limited are the points in Merton's paradigm to 'functional analysis'? Despite the pointing up of functional analysis as a 'special mode' of theorizing, in fact, much of Merton's discussion in this essay ranges far more widely over more general concerns shared by any social analysis (for example, issues about imputing motives to actors). Perhaps, this use of 'functional analysis' to also incorporate more widespread issues in sociology is nicely brought out in a telling passage from Merton's foreword to Johnson's (1960) sociology textbook: "the book does not slavishly conform to a single 'system' of sociology. Instead, it uses the core ideas that today constitute an appreciable working consensus amongst sociologists, whether these ideas are called structural-functional analysis or by some other name". While there is some ambiguity about the extent to which Merton seems to be equating this 'working consensus' with functional analysis, it is clear he goes to no lengths to contrast them (cf. Ben-David, 1978).

(6) What is the relationship between functional and structural analysis? In this essay, Merton speaks mainly of functional analysis, but also uses the phrase "structural and functional analysis" (for example, 1949b [1968b, p. 136] in opening his concluding remarks). This is an interesting usage. Clearly the two are seen as linked, but not in the interpenetrating Parsonian sense, in which the structural analysis describes the 'bones' of the system and the functional analysis 'explains' its operation, in the classic anatomy/physiology metaphor. But nor are they seen as all that loosely connected: note that they are not termed 'structural and functional analysis'.

It does not require much textual analysis to explicate the 'structural analysis' component of Merton's approach. Nevertheless, this aspect is only partially developed by Merton, is not given a consistent terminology, and has been almost totally ignored by commentators. Structural analysis is seen by Merton as the handmaiden to functional analysis, as the preliminary stage on which a subsequent functional analysis is to be built: ". . . Functional analyses begin with a systematic inclusion (and, preferably, charting) of the statuses and social interrelations of those engaging in the behaviour under scrutiny" (1968b, p. 110). And then after an extract from a study concerning the Chiricahua puberty ceremonial for girls, Merton tellingly comments that: ". . . the sheer description' of the ceremony in terms of the statuses and group affiliations of those variously involved provides a major clue to the functions performed by the ceremonial . . . . The structural description of participants in the activity under analysis provides hypotheses for subsequent functional interpretations" (1968b, p. 110).

The task of structural description is to examine the location in the social structure of participants and their pattern of differential participation.

(7) Commentators have also usually missed the conflict perspective built into Merton's postulates that functional alternatives, equivalents or substitutes ought to be examined and that the structural constraints that delimit them should be analysed (postulates 7 and 8, 1968b, p. 106). This is especially emphasized in the Darwinian or Marxian ring of the phrase he uses to describe the relations between the official political structures and political machines: ". . . this struggle between alternative structures for fulfilling the nominally same function" (1968b, p. 129). Some commentators (Wallace, 1969; Nagel, 1956) have noted that the awkward phrase that Merton uses to refer to 'functional alternatives' is ambiguous and would be better replaced with the term 'structural alternatives'. In Stinchcombe's (1968, pp. 80–100) reconstruction of types of causal imagery, the notion that functional analyses focus on the selection amongst alternative structures is central. This creative methodological development of Mertonian functional analysis deserves more attention.

(8) To what extent does Merton identify particular interests of groups? This conflict perspective is further extended by his analysis of the benefits and costs accruing to different groups in relation to the two alternative structures. For example: "For a second subgroup, that of business (primarily 'big' business but also 'small'), the political boss serves the function of providing those political privileges which entail immediate economic gains" (1968b, p. 129). Not only does this form of analysis introduce different groups into the otherwise systems-level analysis, but it brings in the economic interests of these groups.

(9) In any case, it is not entirely clear that Merton has extensively used functional analysis himself. Some evaluation needs to be made of the extent to which Merton's claim is justified that it is ". . . this framework of functional analysis which has variously guided the writing of all the papers in this volume" (1957 edition of Social Theory and Social Structure, p. 11: not included in 1968 edition). The insertion of 'variously' is appropriate, as it is difficult to trace much close-worked use of functional analysis in any strict sense. There seems to be a marked contrast between the examples incisively arrayed in the chapter on 'Manifest and Latent Functions' and the

quite limited deployment of a functional mode of analysis throughout the remainder of the volume.

The degree to which the functional analysis approach is applied can be nicely judged by examining the introductions to each part of the book, which serve to provide an ". . . intellectual passage from one part to the next" (1968b, p. 15). This is a particularly appropriate test of his usage of his functional approach as the introductions would have been written at much the same time as his essay on "Manifest and Latent Functions".

Merton sees his studies,in Part II of *Social Structure and Social Theory,* of the structural sources of deviant behaviour, the bureaucratic structure, the structural bases of the emergence of reference groups, and the social mechanism of the self-fulfilling prophecy as each involving a functional analysis. However, the studies of occupations (the social science expert) and of community influentials, which are also included in this part are more generally referred to as sociological analyses. Indeed, as far as the introduction to Part II is concerned, the substitution of 'structural' for 'functional' would alter the meaning little, and perhaps would fit more easily with the continual use of the term 'structure' in the text, since only in comments noting the dysfunctions of bureaucracies is an identifiable functional mode of analysis actually deployed.

'Function' is mentioned only in passing in the introduction to Part III (in the discussion of the functions of European sociology of knowledge compared to American mass communications research) and not at all in the introduction to Part IV. In sum, it is difficult to see that Merton's claim that his book exemplifies a range of functional analyses is correct. The evidence points more to only a supplementary use of peculiarly functional analyses.

(10) A related question is to attempt to pinpoint the timing of the emergence of this 'functional analysis' approach from whatever theoretical position preceded it in Merton's thinking. The term is included in the subtitle of his work (with Sorokin) on *Social Time* (1937), although it is a general usage, without clear analytical purpose. There is a skeletal functional analysis approach in Merton's doctoral dissertation (published in 1938) — the attention to unintended consequences, and the interest in the interaction between several institutional areas. The attention to unintended consequences was more clearly signalled in his earlier (1936b) essay on this topic, although this does not extend to consequences which affect institutions; and his essay on 'social structure and anomie' has a fleeting discussion in its concluding section of the functions of deviance for the adaptability of social systems. But this 1936 essay is mainly concerned with

the generation by social structure of consequences rather than with their feedback effects of conforming or deviant behaviour for wider structures.

A 1938 letter from Kingsley Davis to Merton offers joint publication of their separate but parallel work on inter-racial marriage, and goes on to suggest that this ". . . might constitute our first exercise in preparation for the more important functionalism collaboration" (1976b, p. 245). This may suggest that this approach was collectively developing within the Harvard environment from which Davis and Merton both emanated. Unfortunately, any reply by Merton in relation to this wider project is not published. However, Turner and Maryanski (1979, p. 61) report that Merton's course in theory while at Harvard (see above, Chapter 2) had been influential in setting the functionalist approach on its feet. The developing framework can be traced in some publications in this period. Merton's study on intermarriage (1941b) does include a short discussion of the functions of endogamy for a social group (by increasing group solidarity) but is mainly a structural account of the differing social sources of types of intermarriage pattern. Writing in 1976, Merton describes this paper as attempting a structural and functional analysis (1976b, p. x) but he also indicates that this identification may involve ". . . some implications not evident at the time of their first writing" (1976b, p. ix). His 1945 review of frameworks in the sociology of knowledge refers to manifest and latent functions imputed to mental productions (ideas), and by this time the use of the term is widespread in his writing.

While the first signs of this recognition of the relevance of the functional approach to sociology appeared in the late 1930s, they seem to have been developed into a more explicit stance only by the mid-1940s alongside his writing of his major essay on functional analysis. (There seems to be a standard account of the birth of functionalism as emanating from Henderson's seminar on systems theory (e.g. Gouldner, 1970), but the direct impact of this seminar on Merton's thinking is quite negligible and this description seems quite inadequate.)

(11) What has been the fate of functional analysis? Merton's essay, together with Davis's textbook and Parsons's emerging theoretical enterprise, led to a sprawling debate about functionalism within sociology. Several eminent philosophers of science analysed the logical adequacy of the procedures, while a variety of social scientists from a range of disciplines debated the merits and demerits of the approach and explored variations within it. The debates raged through the 1950s and the early 1960s (see the useful collection edited by Demerath and Peterson (1967)) and still occasionally splutter into a macabre shortlived dance of wraiths

(Campbell, 1982; Giddens, 1977). But, despite the centrality of Merton's essay in providing the impetus to the debate, it is not particularly productive to try to follow its contorted vicissitudes.

It seems reasonable merely to note that a consensus seems to have grown slowly that functional explanation in its more simple form was fatally flawed by t' ˑ fallacious teleological pseudo-causal mechanism at its heart. However, it is also widely agreed that the debate helped enormously in clarifying some of the opportunities and limitations of social theorizing, and that, despite its severe limits, the functional mode of analysis has considerable heuristic advantages in carrying out analyses because it pushes towards analytical acuity of the aggregate level of social activities. Some contributions to the debate, especially Stinchcombe's (1968) book, have been particularly creative.

Merton's own contribution to the methodological debate on functional approaches is widely felt to have at least two critical problems: that by loosening the tight framework of systemic interdependencies in classic functional analysis, it complicated the logic of this approach, and by introducing individuals (and especially their knowledge and intentions) into the analysis it complicated the level of analysis involved (e.g. Nagel, 1956; Campbell, 1982).

This first point is succinctly made by Dore (1961) when he states that modification of the functional proposition of perfect integration ". . . from 'always perfectly' to 'usually somewhat' integrated (a) destroys the possibility of its empirical falsification and (b) destroys its value as an automatic means of transition from function to cause". Thus, a strictly functional explanation of a totally interlocked set of institutions is possible, but any relaxation from complete interdependence completely undermines this explanatory strategy. The arguably unnecessary inclusion of 'subjective dispositions' was early made in Nagel's formalization of functionalism and he suggests that the distinction is irrelevant to the functional mode of explanation, and others have added that it may precisely be the socially shared understanding of consequences that shapes behaviour with respect to institutional consequences.

The particular irony of Merton's concern to establish a more sound methodological basis for functionalism is that he may have, instead, fatally weakened it!

4.4 MERTON AS A STRUCTURAL ANALYST

At some point between 1968 (when the third edition of *Social Theory and Social Structure* was published) and 1975, Merton shed his 'functional analyst' label to become a 'structural analyst'. (The first clear use of the term 'structural analysis' seems to be in the essay on "Insiders and Outsiders" (1972a, [1973, p. 136]). His 1975 formulation of structural analysis is rather awkwardly described. Merton keeps on referring to ". . . that variant of functional analysis which has evolved, over the years, into a distinct mode of structural analysis" (1976b, p. ix). But as with his paradigm of functional analysis, Merton sketches out a programmatic framework, and also argues a stance in relation to several issues in structural analysis.

I think that in order to explicate Merton's theoretical thinking at this point in his career we need to begin with his very lightly sketched map of different paradigms or theoretical orientations within sociology. He contrasts structural analysis with symbolic interactionism, but sees them as complementary ("like ham and eggs", 1976b, p. 119). Within structural analysis there are various approaches, and Merton contrasts the classical mode of structural-functional analysis with 'this' variant. Merton drives two main contrasts between 'this' variant and that of Parsons — an emphasis on ". . . structural sources and differential consequences of conflict, dysfunctions and contradictions in social structure" (1976b, p. 126) and a commitment to a theoretical pluralism.

But, the thrust of 'this variant of functional analysis' is limited by its lack of a clear imagery, as well as the lack of a name. For once, Merton's keen sense of naming seems to have deserted him, and this terminological lack may be a surface indication of underlying difficulty. So to exorcize this minor problem, I will refer to 'Mertonian structural analysis'.

The features of the Mertonian structural analysis are sketched out through a set of 'stipulations' which (1976b, pp. 120–126):

— emphasize its multiple ancestral lineages of thought;
— locate the main ancestral lineage as a convergence principally drawing from Marx and Durkheim;
— draw attention to the need to span both micro- and macro-level analyses;
— identify the key micro-level process as (explicitly following Stinchcombe) the "choice between socially structured alternatives";
— identify the key macro-level structures as the "social distributions of . . . authority, power, influence and prestige" and the key macro-level processes as involving "cumulation of advantage and disadvantage";
— posit that social structures generate social conflict;
— posit that sociological ambivalence is built into normative structures;
— posit that social structures generate differing rates of deviant behaviour;

— posit that social structures generate change within and of structure itself;
— posit that every new birth cohort modifies social structure as it passes through it;
— posit an analytical difference between manifest and latent levels of social structure;
— admit that structural analysis provides limited explanations.

Merton devotes little space to detailing this approach and gives no examples — in very considerable contrast to the vigour of his earlier essay on functional analysis. Instead, readers are directed to several accounts [Loomis and Loomis (1965), Barbarno (1968), Wallace (1969), Mulkay (1971) and Stinchcombe (1975)] — as ". . . having worked out the essentials of this mode of structural analysis, more deeply and more critically than I am prepared to do" (1975a [1976b, p. 120]).

Interestingly, much of the essay is devoted to arguing a case for sociology as a multi-paradigm discipline. The earlier image of a broad working consensus within sociology, containing a variety of approaches, is shaded over by a picture of sociology as consisting in a small plurality of complementary theoretical orientations. Whereas the earlier functional analysis essay did not draw any contrasts with any non-functional sociology, the later structural analysis essay explicitly suggests that there are other non-structural approaches to sociology.

4.5   COMMENTARY ON MERTON'S STRUCTURAL ANALYSIS

Merton's apparent abandonment of his earlier functional analysis is puzzling. There is no formal withdrawal, and no direct discussion about his clearly widening separation from Parsons's theoretical system. Indeed, the term 'functional analysis' still lurks, unexamined, at a couple of points in the more recent account (". . . it is analytically useful to distinguish between manifest and latent levels of social structure *as of social function*" (1976b, p.126, my emphasis). Nor is there discussion about why the shift in stance was adopted. There seem to be few clues in Merton's own writings, as to the roots of the change. However, the intellectual environment had been changing during the early 1970s with a heightened popularity of the term 'structuralism', while 'functional' analysis was being increasingly subject to critique. An early sign that the 'writing was on the wall' was Kingsley Davis's 1959 Presidential Address to the American Sociological Association on the myth of functional analysis. Davis had earlier been an enthusiastic functional analyst, who had published prominent and controversial functional analyses of prostitution and social stratification as well as a major textbook (*Human Society,* 1948). But in his 1959 address Davis denies any particular virtue in a uniquely functional mode of analysis, and argues that such virtues as functional analysis has had already been incorporated into 'good sociological analysis'. This line of attack has been continued further by other writers, such as Goode (1973) who portrays functionalism as an empty castle, which critics continue to attack, seemingly unaware that the defensive positions have long been abandoned (if indeed they had ever been manned in the first place).

Further clues to the change might be found amongst the writers Merton pointed to. One direct source of influence was a series of articles by an Italian social theorist, Barbano (especially the one translated into English, 1968). Merton himself draws attention to the point that this essay is subtitled "the emancipation of structural analysis in Sociology". Barbarno is particularly concerned to drive a wedge between Mertonian structural analysis and Parsons's structural-functionalism. He seems to centre on the idea that Mertonian structuralism concentrates on the item (what I above termed 'partial functional analysis') rather than the system.

Wallace (1969) makes a similar point in placing the Mertonian mode of analysis in his typology of theoretical approaches as a 'functional structuralism' alongside 'exchange structuralism' and 'conflict structuralism' but well separated from Parsonian 'functional imperativism'. The latter is seen as being concerned with the ways in which social systems are organized to cope with meeting systemic requirements, whereas the three forms of 'structuralism' share an interest in the explanation of social phenomena (patterns of behaviour and social interaction) in terms of the social structure of statuses of participants. The three structuralisms are organized in a hierarchy: ". . . Whereas functional structuralism typically focuses on one side of a given social transaction, exchange structuralism attends to both sides" (Wallace, 1969, p. 28) and 'conflict structuralists' examine situations of unequal exchange in which a benefit is traded for an injury. However, neither of these sources develop their thinking much beyond these sketches.

Examination of the other three references Merton draws attention to gets little further in uncovering any clear models of structural analysis. Loomis and Loomis (1965) label Merton as a structural analyst, but do not debate the point, and otherwise map quite a wide range of Merton's analyses onto their own theoretical schema. Mulkay (1971) provides a clear and critical rendition of functional analysis and anomie theory (but without noticing that the latter draws but very slightly on the methodology sketched out in the former). Stinchcombe (1975) provides a micro-sociological reconstruction of Merton's perspective. It seems that the main point that most of this group of commentators shared (all but Mulkay who discusses Merton's work under the ambiguous heading of 'a second functional alternative') was that Merton is a structural analyst rather than a functional analyst. But they do not then converge in their presentation of what a structuralist approach might involve, despite Merton's apparent faith that they do. (And their accounts are littered with difficulties and mistakes, the exploration or correction of which is largely irrelevant to the task at hand.)

Other sources unacknowledged by Merton may nevertheless have influenced him. Gouldner argues that Merton's approach to a model of a social system ". . . can be regarded as a strategy of minimal commitment" (1959 [1973, p. 192]), and goes on to attempt to develop an underlying model of interchanges between partial structures which he glimpses within Merton's approach: he attempts to promote 'exchange' theory to a collective level, rather than its more usual lodgement at the individual level. Demerath (1967) tries to recast the several decades of the debate over functionalism in terms of the part – whole distinction which he uses to locate differences between Parsons and Merton. And Sztompka (1974) identifies a hierarchy of different layerings of systems thinking in sociology, and describes Merton's approach as falling within a 'functional-motivational' level which incorporates individual purposes. Charles Page's retrospective comment (1982, p. 262) that "Later I became interested . . . by functional doctrine of the Mertonian, not the Parsonian variety . . ." is an indication that the distinction between the two was becoming more widely recognized at this time.

A final and very immediate influence may have come from Peter Blau, a former student of Merton, at the time a colleague, and perhaps most importantly the organizer of the plenary session presentations to the 1974 Conference of the American Sociological Association at which Merton's 1975 essay was presented. The aim of these sessions (and the subsequent collection) was to ". . . juxtapose various theoretical conceptions of structural analysis . . ." (Blau, 1975, p. 2). This context, and the terminology used in it, may have itself exerted some pressure towards the adoption of the structural mode of analysis. This is particularly reinforced by Blau's comment on Merton's community influentials paper that: "Although this paper was published in 1949, the same year as the functional paradigm was, it does not present a functional but a structural explanation of why influential citizens in a community exhibit two contrasting orientations to issues" (1975a, p. 118).

Several of the points Merton makes in the 'stipulations' are interesting. No attempt at all is made to grapple with the offerings of French 'structuralism' which is unfairly dismissed (with negligible direct attention) as something of a newcomer within the broad stream of structural analysis.

Indeed, the parvenu is seen as a "popular and sometimes undiscriminating social movement which has exploited through undisciplined extension the intellectual authority of . . . iconic figures . . ." (1976b, p. 121).

Another interesting point is that in this formulation the 'sacred trio' of sociology's founding fathers is split open, and a pairing of Durkheim and Marx is claimed as the underlying inspiration for structural analysis. Yet this convergence bridges the two founding fathers in a fairly superficial way. And the dropping of Weber is surprising, given the availability of structural readings of Weber (e.g. Turner, 1981) on the one hand, and on the other hand Merton's retention in his framework of structural analysis of Stinch-combe's model of the micro-processes, which strikes me as having a definite Weberian ambience. Surely, Simmel too, deserves a place in the sun as a precursor of structural sociology.

While Merton validates Stinchcombe's interpretation of the micro-processes underlying Mertonian structural analysis, he adds a rather more surprising macro-sociological centre-piece of the accumulation processes that are the mechanisms which build up stratification systems. While the incorporation of more macro-level analysis has been a feature of Mertonian sociology of science there has been relatively little work relating this feature more generally to other social systems.

While several of the points made in his 'stipulations' are interesting, they do not have the power of his earlier framework for functional analysis. This is largely because Merton is posting a framework around structural analysis, rather than capturing its core through a clear statement of how a structural analysis might be accomplished. Perhaps it is this lack of specificity that has meant that reaction to this later essay has been negligible.

4.6 SOCIOLOGICAL AMBIVALENCE AND SOCIAL PSYCHOLOGY

At different points in his career, Merton sported two other fairly prominent labels. During the 1940s in particular many of his titles and writings included the term 'social psychology', and then from the mid-1950s through to the mid-1970s a theme has been 'sociological ambivalence'.

It is something of a puzzle that for a period in the 1940s some of Merton's writing was under the rubric of 'social psychology'. This extended into the 1960s under a slightly different phrase of 'psychosociological mechanisms', which appears to be a continuity. At first blush, this appears strange, given that this spans the period of his strongest commitment to functional analysis.

This interest actually involves a rather different approach to the usual way in which we might now view social psychology. For Merton, as for Gerth and Mills: "To a large extent, then, use of the term is a way of indicating an interest in the social meanings of institutions, as well as the interaction between 'social character' and social context" (Merton, 1953). This approach was adopted in the context of a more widespread interest in social psychology amongst Merton's peers. Gerth and Mills developed their complex institutional analysis around 'social psychology'. Parsons, during this period, was particularly interested in Freud and put himself through psychoanalysis. It may have been politic, too, to attempt to gain an audience within the social psychology wing of the rather larger neighbouring discipline of Psychology.

In several essays written in the mid-1950s (including his "Preliminaries to a Sociology of Medical Education" and his "Priorities in Scientific Discovery" paper: 1957a, 1957c) Merton noted that ambivalences arose as individuals were subject to various forms of cross-pressure from the complex social structure which they were placed in. In 1963 this theme was taken up in an essay (written with Elinor Barber) on 'social ambivalence' (more correctly 'social ambivalence'?) which ten years later became the anchoring-point for several other inquiries all collected into one part of his book with this title (1976b).

He suggests that the core-type of ambivalence involves ambivalence being embedded in particular statuses and status-sets, together with their associated roles (1963a [1976b, p. 7]), but also in rather different language that ". . . the major norms and minor counter-norms alternatively govern role-behaviour to produce ambivalence" (1963a [1976b, p. 17]).

Merton then lists a hierarchical series of different types of ambivalence:

— (in the most restricted sense) it is the ". . . incompatible normative expectations incorporated in a single role of a single social status (for example, the therapist role of the physician as distinct from other roles of his or her status as researcher, administrator, professional colleague, participant in the professional association, etc.)" (1976b, p. 6);
— conflicts of interest or values between different statuses (i.e. status-set) occupied by a single person;
— conflict between several roles associated with a particular status (e.g. between teaching, research, administration etc. for a university person or scientist);
— contradictory cultural values (e.g. sacred family values v. business needs);
— ". . . disjunction between culturally prescribed aspirations and socially structured avenues for realising these aspirations" (1976b, p. 11);

— 'marginal men' (such as immigrants or more generally the socially mobile) who have been subject to two sets of cultural values (in sequence, or through holding a reference orientation to a group of which one is not a member).

It is difficult to be sure how far Merton intends his conception of 'sociological ambivalence' to be incorporated within his overall work. While his essay on sociological ambivalence gives the title for his third volume of collected papers, and leads a series of essays and part-essays that explore the workings of sociological ambivalence in various institutional areas, the more widespread pertinence of this theme is circumscribed by the doleful tacking of "and other essays" to the volume title, which protects the essays collected in the two other parts of the volume. It is clear that it conveys an important image of social reality, that ambivalence is built into the complex way social structures are constructed, as opposed to images that social reality is a smooth facade of consensus, riven by competition or rent by conflict. In presenting this image, Merton distances himself from Parsons who has indicated that, in his understanding, societies can only tolerate a very limited amount of ambivalence and strain. Further, the discussion of sociological ambivalence serves to summarize several themes that run through Merton's writings:

— the importance of maintaining an interest in the experiental psychological level of analysis, while focusing particularly on the social structural contexts of that level;
— the varying ways and levels in which cultural and social structures are arranged and are variously integrated and malintegrated;
— the varying ways in which ambivalences flow from divergent tendencies in sets of cultural goals (and counter-goals) and are then amplified or contracted by structural means;
— the continuity between conformity and change;
— the consequences for institutional structures of the ambivalences they generate, through the amplification and diffusion of components of ambivalence.

But beyond this reiteration and repackaging of points developed elsewhere there remains a difficulty about where exactly this concept of ambivalence is to be located, theoretically. It seems to me perhaps best treated as a perspective on the 'dependent variables' likely to pertain in any sociological analysis, together with something of a guide to likely lines of theoretical explanation of these. Merton, perhaps characteristically and ironically, is ambivalent on this point.

This conception appears not to have been widely taken up, although Room (1976) discusses its relevance to the explanation of alcohol problems: albeit to little effect.

4.7 CONCLUSION

It seems, then, that Merton's own elucidations of his theoretical position may be rather too limited to explain his impact on American sociology. It seems necessary to construct an account by digging behind and codifying Merton's own studies to show 'how they work'. After all, given Merton's own methodological proscription on general theories it is not surprising that he has not himself clarified this aspect of his work. An adaptation of his own remarks when commenting on a paper by historian of science Rupert Hall exactly sums up my attitude towards Merton's own statements of his theoretical contributions to sociology:

> [Merton] sets out the essentials of his discussion in [several] succinct [categories and stipulations]. It would therefore seem that my work is largely done. Indeed, it would be, if I were to accept [Merton's] synopsis as adequate. But I do not. Excellent as the synopsis is in so many ways, it does not begin to do justice to [his work], to its richness of content, its subtlety of analysis, and its variety of implications. (I do not hesitate to differ with [Merton] on this score; after all, he only wrote [it]; I have studied it) (1959c, p. 24).

5

Merton's general theory II: latent theoretical stance

The previous chapter has shown the difficulties in Merton's own definition of his contribution to social theory. Yet, Merton had in fact developed his own particular analytical apparatus, applied in a series of analyses and partly drawn out in developing theoretical articulations. But this general framework has never been explicitly developed by Merton himself. Indeed, the very idea of having a general theoretical framework would be denied by his methodological doctrines on 'middle-range' theory, and his opposition to premature general social theories. Stinchcombe directly raises this difficulty and openly clashes with Merton's own theoretical modesty. Stinchcombe argues that:

> I do not agree with Merton's implicit diagnosis [of the usefulness of his theories] that it is because he works on 'theories of the middle range'. It seems to me that in the dialectic between Parsons and Merton, generality has been confused with woolliness. Merton, in taking up the correct position on woolliness, has tricked himself into taking up the incorrect position on general theory. The true situation is precisely the opposite. It is because Merton has a better general theory than Parsons that his work has been more empirically fruitful (Stinchcombe, 1975, pp. 26, 27).

5.1 STINCHCOMBE'S MODEL OF MERTON

Attention to this underlying analytical apparatus was first drawn in a penetrating exposition by Arthur Stinchcombe (1975). Stinchcombe goes on to codify the key elements of this Mertonian theory of social structure. In further work, Stinchcombe is able to show that a similar model can be found embedded in the analyses of Tocqueville, Lenin and Bendix (Stinchcombe, 1978), although he himself chooses not to stress this continuity (he does not refer to his earlier essay on Merton in his book devoted to this trio).

I begin by summarizing Stinchcombe's reconstruction, but because it does not adequately cover enough of Merton's working model, I then extend it further in the remainder of this chapter.

The Stinchcombe version of the model centres on variation between people in their rates of choice amongst alternatives which are structurally produced, and in which the rates of choice loop back to affect the institutional patterns which had shaped the rates of choice 'in the first place'. People differ in their rates of choice amongst structurally given alternatives depending on their location in the social order. On the one hand, choices are causally structured, and on the other hand, choices causally influence the development of institutional patterns: the causal chain goes backwards and also forwards from the core process as the key-phrase of 'choices with institutional consequence' nicely points up.

For example, as Merton has shown, scientists are particularly concerned with the publication of research reports of original investigations, and the institutional pattern of science supports and motivates this. In turn, the importance of open publication rather than secrecy, and the continued availability of journals to publish in, is enhanced when scientists choose to publish their research work.

The key relationships in Stinchcombe's model can be usefully sketched (see Fig. 3; cf. Stinchcombe, 1975, p. 13).

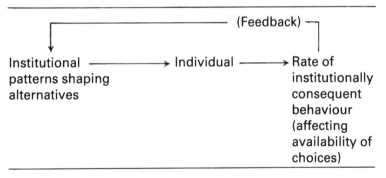

Fig. 3 — Basics of Stinchcombe's model of Merton's analyses.

Stinchcombe then thickens out this account by identifying three particular ways through which institutional patterns shape individual choice behaviour (through structurally induced motives, control of information and sanctions), and also a causal loop in which the development of social character is influenced by choices and in turn affects the ways choices are made.

The first part of Stinchcombe's extension of the core model provides more detail about how Merton's theoretical work explains the linkage between institutional pattern and individual rates of choice. People in different social positions will have different goals or motivations, stemming from some mix of a range of structural sources — the cultural beliefs they have been socialized into, reward systems (including the striving after status), seeking to affirm social identities valued by reference groups, and the need to maintain everyday life.

Another key mechanism linking institutional pattern and individual choice behaviour is the structural governance of information. The availability of information influences the knowledge of the range of choice (as well as, presumably, the person's weighing up of the costs and benefits of each alternative they are aware of). The flow of information may itself be a resource that affects the success in carrying out an activity (and in turn, success reinforces the choice of continuing in that activity). And the application of sanctions (rewards and punishments) is dependent on knowing when and whom to reward or punish.

Further, a person's choice behaviour may be influenced by the social pressure which others bring to bear on them through their ability to reward or punish the person.

The last component which Stinchcombe adds into the model is a feedback loop involving socially patterned character or personality development. As a result of being placed in a particular social situation (for example, a bureaucrat), and making repeated similar choices, a particular social character is formed. This is further reinforced as it influences the style in which choice behaviour is carried out, which limits a person's exposure to alternative sources of information or social pressure. Thus a style of operating becomes cemented in.

In this analytical reconstruction, Stinchcombe usefully draws on a wide range of Merton's specific analyses: especially the essay on anomie, but also Merton's analyses of bureaucracy, behaviour amongst scientists, the political machine, the cosmopolitan/local distinction and his analysis of the structural position of engineers. However, a range of other work by Merton, and especially his more theoretical essays, are only lightly drawn on. There is little to fault in what Stinchcombe says about Merton's work: indeed, there is a complimentary, if passing, endorsement of it by Merton, (1976, pp. 120, 124) who notes that Stinchcombe's model is couched at a particularly analytical level, but specifies that it only reconstructs the micro-processes underlying Mertonian structural analysis. However, there is some difficulty with what Stinchcombe does not say, and a need to scour more widely through Merton's theoretical writings to include relevant theoretical material.

5.2   AN EXTENDED STRUCTURAL MODEL OF MERTON

Stinchcombe's account, consonant with his earlier 'theory-constructionist' approach (Stinchcombe, 1968) stresses processes rather than structures. He is rather too ready to show how Merton sees the 'social machine' as working, and not careful enough to show how Merton sees the components and organization of the 'social machine' in the first place. Along with this is an overemphasis on the micro-sociological or social psychological components rather than structural levels of analysis. Yet, Merton is a theorist particularly concerned with the essential properties and types of social structure, as well as the detailed ways in which they work. The exposition of Merton's theory of social structure which follows is intended to complement and extend the basic insights laid out by Stinchcombe. His work should be able to be neatly located within my broader model.

There are five key elements in this extended version of Stinchcombe's core model. Two of the elements in his model are repeated, one is new, while the other two consist of a subdivision of one of his elements. I also develop the mapping of relationships amongst these elements.

Choice of starting point in presentation is arbitrary. Perhaps it is easiest to begin with the individual choosing amongst alternatives on the one hand, and linked to this, patterns of behaviour resulting from these choices. In this I follow Stinchcombe's presentation, although relaxing somewhat his narrowing of patterns of behaviour to only those which are consequent for institutions: it seems to me important to attempt to retain the analytical possibility (laid out in the concept of 'non-functional consequences' in Merton 1949b [1968b, p. 105]) that not all behaviour patterns are institutionally consequent (cf. Boudon, 1981).

Where I depart from Stinchcombe rather more substantially is in building forward from choices into Merton's views of the social environment shaping those choices. The social environment needs to be subdivided into 'cultural structure' and 'social structure'. A brief textual analysis can readily substantiate that Merton used these terms to represent quite different aspects of social reality. Broadly, cultural structure consists in the shared ideas which shape people's images of social reality, provide motivations and ideological justifications for institutional patterns and cultural products. On the other hand, social structures are patterned social relationships amongst people. Social structures mediate between cultural patterns and the behaviour patterns resulting from choices. Whereas the cultural structure provides goals (albeit selectively reinforced by social arrangements), social structure provides the means for making and implementing choices. (As Merton points out, there may be marked disjunctions between aspects of cultural and social structures, and congruence should not be assumed.)

To a considerable extent, this distinction between cultural and social structural elements repeats the orthodox introductory sociology textbook exposition (although this of course is not uninfluenced by Merton!). Nevertheless, it is a useful distinction. One of Merton's major theoretical accomplishments was a systematic codification of how to go about analysing cultural and social structures, as well as analysing their linkage to behaviour patterns.

A related aspect of many of Merton's analyses which Stinchcombe under-emphasizes is the three-layer model in which macro-structures, especially social class, are seen 'working behind', and through, intermediate social structures to influence social practices. While it is difficult to formally implement this in the extended model, I will attempt to generally draw attention to this central aspect.

In his earlier writing, Merton did not give much attention to the micro-contexts of interaction in which people's behaviour is set. However, this is explicitly addressed in his later work, and so will be treated as a separate element in the extended model. His most recent theoretical writings have featured analysis of 'socially expected durations', and this will receive discrete attention.

Finally, in dealing with the consequences of behaviour for the maintenance and change of the institutional structures (which induce and shape the behaviour in the first place) an important distinction which is buried within Stinchcombe's reconstruction and the above diagram must be brought out. Behaviour will have consequences not only for the institutional structures in which it is directly embedded, but also for other institutional structures. An obvious example of this is the 'Merton thesis' that the Puritan ethos legitimated a concern with nature and technology. So, 'feedback' effects need to be separated from 'leakage' effects. Both are likely to be usually unintended and unanticipated, but feedback effects particularly so. An outline of the more structural framework I will employ is shown in Fig. 4.

5.3 BOUNDARIES OF SOCIAL PHENOMENA

Before going on to examine Merton's analytical system, some attention needs to be directed towards identifying its boundaries. Like other social theorists, Merton demarcates those features of human existence which are amenable to social inquiry from other features which are seen to be below

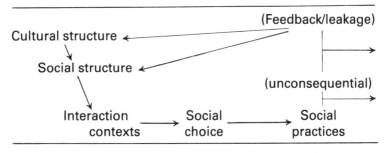

Fig. 4 — Extended model.

the threshold of sociological attention. Whereas Weber contrasted 'meaningful' behaviour with mere biological behaviour, Merton demarcates between ". . . standardized (i.e. patterned and repetitive)" (1968b, p. 104) and presumably rather more ephemeral and idiosyncratic 'forms' or levels of activity. The units of analysis are expected to exhibit a degree of 'institutionalization' of behaviour, although it is explicitly held that social patterns may include aspects that need to be observed as they are not culturally recognized, or recognized by the participants. It is, unfortunately, unclear as to what is involved with this residue of 'non-institutionalised (collective?) behaviour' or how it might be analysed. (Merton has had no particular occasion to address the analytical issues of what social phenomena outside this definition might involve. He does not do so in his nearest attempt when writing an introduction [1960] to Le Bon's book on crowds. Instead, he provides an unjustly unknown *tour de force* in which Freud's reaction to Le Bon's analysis is examined.)

However, he does begin an analysis of the interaction between institutional and 'pre-institutional' levels of social behaviour in his commentary on the effect of the self-fulfilling prophecy when rushes on banks result in the very bank failures which investors fear (1948d [1968b, pp. 476, 477]). In discussing this Merton notes that "The self-fulfilling prophecy, whereby fears are translated into reality, operates only in the absence of deliberate institutional controls" (1968b, p. 490).

Stinchcombe adds to this definition, the criterion that in order to be of sociological interest social phenomena should be 'institutionally consequent'. This adds slightly to Merton's definition, by increasing the theoretical depth of interpretation. Stinchcombe's point emphasizes the double-sided nature of social phenomena — they are both caused by social structure, and result in reproducing social structure. Thus, for example, in considering the choice of a political party to vote for, the range of choice amongst parties and even the possibility of voting are both affected by social structure, and in turn the act of choosing a particular party will have consequences in terms of the continued viability of that party and of the voting system more generally.

5.4 CULTURAL STRUCTURE

For Merton, as for Durkheim, culture is a collective phenomenon imposing on people externally, but also carried by them. "Cultural structure may be defined as that organized set of normative values governing behaviour which is common to members of a designated society or group" (1968b, p. 216).

Merton's model of cultural structure is not particularly sophisticated, and (as in Weber's analyses of cultural structures such as *The Protestant Ethic and the Spirit of Capitalism*) is conducted with a very considerable eye to the social consequences of beliefs, or knowledge or values. This contrasts with more analytical concerns with the internal interrelationships within cultural structures themselves which so dominate the attention of French 'structuralists', and a variety of other more recent approaches in social theory. Nevertheless, there are several crucial distinctions which Merton deploys in constructing descriptions of cultural structures.

A major distinction is made between 'core-values' (also variously expressed as 'Creed' [in the analysis of American race ideologies] or 'Code' [in the analysis of the value-structure of pure science] or 'Cultural Goals' [in relation to the 'American dream']) and 'institutional norms', which are the more detailed forms in which the core values are 'operationalized' to influence social behaviour.

Much emphasis is placed on the built-in complexity of normative structures. This can be portrayed as patterns of norms and counter-norms, in which each norm is 'balanced' by its opposite, although the two seldom receive equal weighting. Reference is made to the hierarchical ordering of the importance of values and norms, but procedures for examining this aspect of cultural structure are not developed (however, compare "Studies in Radio and Film Propaganda" (1943b [1968b, pp. 563–582]) and the discussion of Holton's conception of 'themata': 1975b).

Another distinction is made between the more technical and the more social components of cultural structure. The former covers beliefs, knowledge and values concerning material production and the last concerns, beliefs, knowledge and values in relation to social structure. In an early essay Merton used Alfred Weber's pair of terms 'civilization' and 'culture' to differentiate between these two aspects. However, this nomenclature was subsequently downplayed (although briefly footnoted in 1968b, p. 24), even though the conceptual distinction is continued unremarked in some actual analyses.

Merton argued that these two different aspects of culture are each governed by rather different 'laws', and especially that the former has a capacity to cumulate in ways that the latter is resistant to. This distinction recurs later in Merton's work in his discussions of differences in the growth patterns of the natural sciences compared to the social sciences.

Part of the relative lack of sophistication in his treatment of cultural structure arises in the absence of a clear suggested methodology for investigating it. In actual analyses, Merton is quite careful to attempt to provide an empirical basis in his descriptions of cultural structures, so that it is possible to extract something of a methodology. This is accomplished through quotation from written comments, and to a lesser extent through the citation of 'commonplace sayings'. This, of course, is similar to Weber's approach to the same methodological problem. The sociological justification of this approach flows in large part from the recognition of the importance of pronouncements by key cultural entrepreneurs in affecting the beliefs of others. As well, it has the practical advantages of convenience, and perhaps even the advantage of allowing the display of an apparently almost effortless erudition! Although he himself seldom used survey data on attitude-structures (with the exception of his study using ethnic 'opinionnaires': 1939b) he cites with approval such studies carried out by others. However, it is important to Merton that the empirical studies be carefully carried out: they should particularly attempt to measure individual's perceptions of commonly held cultural values rather than necessarily the individual's own values (see Merton's critical comments [1976b, pp. 59–61] on Mitroff's sins in this regard, as opposed to his earlier unremarked citation of an earlier study by Mitroff: Merton, 1976b, p. 125).

Much of Merton's interest in sociology of knowledge was an attempt to explore the relationships between culture and social structure, but this was largely confined to review work. Given Merton's sustained interest in the sociology of knowledge it must be a continuing disappointment that this area has been slow to seed a cumulation of middle-range theories (cf. Barber, 1975). However, some of Merton's review is pregnant with rich possibilities, when he suggests the hypotheses:

> that societies with sharp social cleavages, as allegedly in France, are more likely to cultivate sociology intensively than societies with a long history of a more nearly uniform value-system, as allegedly in England; that a rising social class is constrained to see the social reality more authentically than a class long in power but now on the way out; that an

upper class will focus on the static aspects of society and a lower one on its dynamic, changing aspects; that an upper class will be alert to the functions of existing social arrangements and a lower class to their dysfunctions; or . . . that socially conservative groups hold to multiple-factor doctrines of historical causation and socially radical groups to monistic doctrines (1961b [1973, pp. 47, 48]).

5.5 SOCIAL STRUCTURE

Merton has a strongly developed analytical approach to social structure. This is organized around the key concepts of status-set and role-set, but also includes attention to characteristics of membership groups, reference-groups, status-sequences and role-sequences and opportunity-structures. Social structure is defined (in contrast to culture) as ". . . that organized set of social relationships in which members of the society or group are variously implicated" (1968b, p. 216).

The boundary between cultural and social structures is not entirely clear, and there is some ambiguity in Merton's various writings on this point. Cole (1979, pp. 74–76) declares that norms belong in social structure whereas other aspects such as the meanings which people attach to social activities lie in culture. It seems important to avoid reifying analytical distinctions. It may, however, be more useful to think of norms as spanning both culture and social structure, with culture providing an array of norms amongst which the social structure selects and then puts its selection into operation through frameworks of reward and constraint.

The central place of status-sets and role-sets is not entirely apparent in the architecture of Merton's published writings. These two key concepts are developed relatively late in his intellectual career (the mid-1950s) and are backed into his extended discussion of reference-groups, as part of a discussion of the structural contexts of reference-groups. (Indeed, whereas status-and-role theory is part of Merton's reference-group theory, I would prefer to reverse the emphasis and make reference-group theory a consequent set of ideas about how status-and-role structures actually work.) However, Merton has otherwise signalled the importance of these analytical tools:

— by a separate article published in the *British Journal of Sociology* (Merton, 1957b);
— by reasonably extended reference to them as examples of 'middle-range' theories in his introductory chapters of *Social Theory and Social Structure;*

— and using these two concepts in the title of an unpublished manuscript, subtitled: 'Structural analysis in sociology' (referred to in 1973, p. 501).

The concepts of status-set and role-set are developments of the general conception of 'status' and 'role' that were expounded by Linton (a major anthropological writer of the 1930s). "By status Linton meant a position in a social system occupied by designated individuals; by role, the behaviour enacting of the patterned expectations attributed to that position" (Merton, 1968b, p. 422). Essentially a status involves a bundle of cultural expectations which guide the actual practice of social relationships amongst social positions which comprise social structure.

The concept of a status-set refers to Linton's point that people occupy multiple statuses, or in Merton's definition it refers to ". . . the complex of distinct positions assigned to individuals both within and among social systems" (1968b, p. 434), for example "the distinct statuses of teacher, wife, mother, Catholic, Republican, and so on" (1968b, p. 423).

Merton briefly develops one implication of his conception of status-sets — the problems they pose to the individual in articulating his or her status-set. The extent of difficulty is seen to vary with the complexity of the status-set.

Various social mechanisms that assist in articulating status-sets are noted:

— perception by others in the status-set of competing obligations (for example, employees are to a degree recognized to have families);
— shared agreement on the relative importance of conflicting status-obligations;
— self-selection of successive statuses that lessen differences between the values learned in earlier-held statuses and those pertaining in later statuses;
— self-selection of statuses which are 'neutral' to one another.

Status-sets are seen as neither randomly sorted nor fully and tightly integrated, although the structural sources of the degree of integration are only briefly explored (see Cole, 1979, pp. 204–206). Social structures are seen as likely to evolve norms and other mechanisms that will assist in articulating status-sets. This is related to the significance of status-sets as a mechanism through which different institutional areas of society are linked, in the person of individuals.

The related concept of status-sequence: a ". . . succession of statuses through which an appreciable proportion of people move" (1968b, p. 436) is also advanced (in part, being pinpointed as a mechanism through which status-sets are articulated). This allows a more precise translation of the distinction between achieved and ascribed statuses: these are different forms of status-sequence.

The conception of role-set is rather more innovative. Merton takes the widely used concept of role, and gives it a strong, useful social structural twist. Whereas Linton saw each status being matched by a single role, Merton suggests that it is analytically more fruitful to conceptualize each status as comprising an array of roles, which is jointly played out in relation to several types of complements to the status (and which is collectively termed the role-set). The concept of role-set is defined, and then described as:

> ... that complement of role relationships which persons have by virtue of occupying a particular social status. As one example, the single status of medical student entails not only the role of a student in relation to his teachers, but also an array of other roles relating the occupant of that status to other students, physicians, social workers, medical technicians, etc. (1968b, p. 423).

The concept is rather more complicated than some analysts have realized since role-set refers not to the 'sub-statuses' constituting the status, but to the other positions/roles which the status-occupant relates to. This relationship can be illustrated as Fig. 5 (cf. Cole, 1979, p. 58). Having indicated this

Status	Role	Role-set
University teacher	Teacher Researcher Administrator	Student Colleagues Bureaucracy
'Housewife'	Mother Wife Relative	Children Husband In-laws
. . .	. . .	. . .

Fig. 5 — Illustration of status-role analysis.

complexity, Merton points to the structural sources of instability in role-sets, and the social mechanisms for the articulation of roles in a role-set.

Since the values and expectations of the role-partners will differ, the individual occupying any status will face disparate, inconsistent and conflicting role-expectations. Interestingly this inconsistency is seen as often welling up from the different social and economic strata within which various role-partners are located (for example, in relation to a teacher, the social background of fellow-teachers as opposed to school board members), and increasing with the diversity of strata locations from which role-partners are drawn. As he points out in his article (but does not then incorporate in *Social Theory and Social Structure*): "It is after all, one of the principal assumptions of Marxist theory as it is of all sociological theory: social differentiation generates distinct interests amongst those variously located in the structure of society" (1957a, p. 112).

A variety of social mechanisms help to articulate role-sets (1968b, pp. 425–433):

— differing intensity of role-involvement among those in the role-set (some role-relationships are central and others peripheral);
— differences in the power of those involved in a role-set;
— insulating role-activities from observability by members of the role-set;
— observability by members of the role-set of their conflicting demands upon the occupants of a social status (this mechanism offsets 'pluralistic ignorance': the situation of unawareness of the extent to which values are in fact shared);
— social support by others in similar social statuses and thus with similar difficulties in coping with an unintegrated role-set;
— abridging the role-set (breaking off particular role-relationships).

As well as providing for the examination of structured relationships between statuses, Merton attempts to analyse the emerging properties of social groups or groupings which are built out of particular types of statuses. Embedded within his discussion of reference-group theory, Merton provides an attempt to sketch out a sociological analysis of membership groups. This is accomplished through an examination of the characteristics of group membership and through the listing of 26 properties groups are considered to possess. This discussion is recognized as an ad hoc and tentative stocktaking. But it is interesting that Merton avoids any premature attempt to develop a classification of types of groups, in order to first clarify the characteristics of groups in general.

Merton does not provide an easy transition between his theory of status-

and role-sets and his theory of groups, except for a clue in a footnote to his later essay on sociological ambivalence. It is noted there that: "role-attributes are in some respects similar to properties of groups which are, after all, organized in the form of interrelated statuses and associated roles" (1976b, p. 17, footnote 31).

Merton distinguishes between three different types of social formation: groups, collectivities and social categories. Social categories are aggregates of social statuses, the occupants of which are not in social interaction. These have like social characteristics — of sex, age, marital condition, income and so on — but are not necessarily orientated toward a distinctive and common body of norms. Having like statuses and, consequently, similar interests and values, social categories can be mobilized into collectivities or into groups (1968b, pp. 353, 354). Collectivities are ". . . people who have a sense of solidarity by virtue of sharing common values and who have acquired an attendant sense of moral obligation to fulfill role-expectations" (1968b, p. 353) and in turn have a potential for group formation. A group is ". . . a number of people who interact with one another in accord with established patterns" (1968b, p. 339), and in addition who define themselves as members and are defined by others as belonging to the group. Thus, groups have both objective (interaction) and subjective (social definition) aspects. This can be assembled (although Merton does not do so) into Fig. 6.

	Subjective		
	Similar norms (Shared status)	Common norms	Shared definition and interaction
Group	X	X	X
Collectively	X	X	
Category	X		

Fig. 6 — Characteristics of three levels of social groupings.

Merton also refers to 'non-membership groups' which are, essentially, the recruitment-base for a group — sharing criteria of eligibility without actually being members. He continues his analysis of groups by listing their main properties (see Fig. 7; 1968b, pp. 364–380). The imagery behind the listing, which many of the posited dimensions point up, is of emergent group properties (properties not inherent in the individuals belonging to the group). These constitute an interplay between the extent to which members are involved in groups on the one hand, and on the other hand the

clarity/vagueness of social definitions of membership in the group
degree of (culturally prescribed) engagement of members in the group
actual (and expected) duration of membership in the group
actual (and expected) duration of the group
absolute (and relative) size of a group, or of component parts of a group
open/closed character of the group
"completeness" (ratio of actual to potential members)
degree of social differentiation
shape and height of stratification
type and degrees of social cohesion
the potential of fission/unity of a group
extent of social interaction within the group
character of social relations obtaining in the group
degree of expected conformity to norms of group (toleration of deviant
behaviour and institutionalized departures from the strict definition of
group-norms)
system of normative controls
degree of visibility/observability within the group
ecological structure of the group
autonomy/dependence of the group
degree of stability of the group
degree of stability of the structural context of the group
modes of maintaining stability of the group (and in relation to the structural
context)
relative social standing of groups
relative power of groups.

Fig. 7 — List of group characteristics.

capacity of the group to command the behaviour of its members in the short-term, and in the long-term to change in reaction to changing circumstances, respond to the wider social environment and so forth. Unfortunately, this approach is not linked to the terminology advanced in the useful Lazarsfeld and Menzel methodological essay (1961) on individual and group properties, although it is probably influenced by it. More systematic use of their typology of types of properties might have substructured this otherwise ad hoc listing. (For similar criticisms see Bierstedt, 1981, p. 482.)

Having provided a conceptual framework for describing the various elements of social structure, Merton then deploys a variety of conceptual frameworks which provide analytical purchase on how the social structure works, and especially, how it connects up with patterns of behaviour. The most well-known of these is 'reference-group theory' (first formulated by Herbert Hyman), but I have also located several other related theories.

Merton's reference-group theory is an attempt to show the mechanisms through which groups shape the behaviour of members. Perhaps the more interesting aspect, which Merton points up, is the way people are influenced by groups they are not members of and even by non-groups!

(that is, fictional groups). What is sociologically problematic is not so much that individuals are affected by social frames of reference, but which particular frames of reference are relevant in influencing them. In order to focus on this issue, Merton sifts through a plethora of scene-setting preliminary conceptual clarification of the way individuals are linked to groups:

— in-group v. out-group
— groups v. quasi-groups or non-groups
— positive v. negative groups
— reference groups v. reference individuals
— membership v. non-membership groups
— normative v. evaluative contexts.

The theory of reference-groups consists in a scatter of propositions, for example:

— "non-membership groups are more likely to be adopted as reference groups in those social systems having high rates of mobility than in those which are relatively closed" (1968b, p. 347), because in open systems such an orientation is more likely to be rewarded by membership;
— increasing intensity of in-group solidarity is often associated with hostility to out-groups, although the opposite process of allegiance to out-groups is even more sociologically interesting (1968b, p. 352);
— individuals wishing to affiliate with a group are likely to adopt its values (1968b, p. 359): [designated 'anticipatory socialization'];
— isolates in a group are more likely to adopt values of non-membership groups than those who are more centrally situated (1968b, p. 359);
— "group affiliations which are matters of achievement, rather than of social ascription, tend to be more often relevant for the acceptance of values . . ." amongst the upwardly mobile (1968b, p. 383).

Another feature of Merton's conception of social structure is that it is a framework around which there is built social distributions of resources — he specifically notes authority, power, influence and prestige (1976a, p. 124) and more generally means for achieving legitimate or illegitimate goals. The concept of "opportunity-structure" (developed by Merton but particularly taken up by Cloward) also points to these social distributions of resources. This aspect of his work was particularly pointed up in his early essay on bureaucracy (1939a [1968b, pp. 250–251]) which makes the Marxian point (extended with a Weberian twist to cover wider arenas of social activity than the economy) that: "With increasing bureacratization, it becomes plain to all who would see that man is to a very important degree controlled by his social relations to the instruments of production. . . . One must be employed by the bureaucracies in order to have access to tools in order to work in order to live". Similar comments are made about the operation of 'Big Science' (Merton, 1973), and more generally in later work on patterns of accumulation of advantage and disadvantage.

An important property of social structures is the extent to which they shape information flows. As Stinchcombe points out "Many of Merton's central concepts have to do with information" (1975, p. 20). He summarizes these as involving three major mechanisms (cf. Merton, 1968b, pp. 373–376):

First, sanctions depend on information. One person cannot sanction another for something he or she does not know the other has done. Second, information affects people's ideas about what choices they are confronted with. People do not choose alternatives they do not know about. Third, people use information in the concrete construction of successful activities, and success in an activity makes the activity more likely to continue. The collective competence of a science to solve scientific problems would be impossible if scientists could not find out the answers of other scientists to their questions (1975, pp. 20, 21).

The way in which social structures motivate people through their reward-structures is important in Mertonian analyses. Indeed, one of the central questions Merton poses in any context is to examine what kinds of signals for effort are given, and also what pointers of displeasure are conveyed so that the likely consequences for different categories of actors can be assessed. This is always a complex situation, as people's behaviour is not totally determined by reward-structures but is mediated by their position in the social structure.

Alongside this concern with the way in which motivation for behaviour is shaped by reward-strutures Merton places ideas about the way in which behaviour is constrained by mechanisms of social control. He has nicely pointed up the variability in the extent to which social norms are socially enforced in his alliterative formula of the 4Ps: prescription, preference, permission and proscription (1968b, p. 187).

Merton has developed a theory of power, or more precisely, a theory of the maintenance and operation of power once structural power has been established. This stresses that authority is, in general, accorded by those who are prepared to obey as the exercise of power must meet with compliance. This in turn means that leaders must be sensitive to the norms of the group and have considerable information about the norms and group operation. Thus leaders are ironically perhaps more trapped in the ongoing structure than their followers. However, leaders have a further responsibility to ensure adaptation to changes to secure long-term survival of the group, and this requires them to initiate or at least support change. But certainly, in Merton's theory, power is seen as necessary coordination function and a social resource whose exercise is closely limited by the followers. This is an image of power that operates only within a general consensus of values — however unenthusiastically held — and does not recognize a role for the application of violence which many other analysts see as a significant resource which underlies the wielding of power in at least some extreme contexts.

Finally, the various more technically analytical aspects of Merton's social structural theory can be set within a broader imagery of levels of social structure, and its overall mode of operation.

Social structure is seen as being divided into two levels:

— the larger social structure (for example, the class or political structure of a society); and
— the social milieu (the patterns of interpersonal relations in which individuals are directly involved: 1955, pp. 26, 27).

The pressures of the larger social structure are mediated through this social milieu. Merton suggests that there is a tendency in sociology to concentrate on the milieu, if only because of an interest in the meanings articulated by actors, which leads to a relative neglect of the larger social structure. This is an interesting comment, given that Merton's emphasis often is on milieu rather than the larger structure (see 1973, p. 374).

But despite this emphasis, both structural levels are involved in many Mertonian analyses: for example, in examining role conflict he points to difficulties which might arise from the different social backgrounds of different members of the role-set; and in his analysis of deviance different social class situations are more likely to lead to particular modes of adaptation. It is a central feature of Merton's sociology that he 'connects up' macro-structure with more immediate social organization, and one of the prime analytical strengths of status-and-role theory is that it provides an understanding of the intervening channels through which macro-structures shape behaviour. (This linkage is particularly pointed up in the quotation used above, Chapter 3, that links characteristics of European sociologists of knowledge with American attitude surveyors.)

Either milieu or larger social structures may be characterized as being in a condition of organization, disorganization or unorganization. "In unorganization a system of social relations has not yet evolved, while in disorganization acute or chronic disruptions occur in a more or less established system of social relations" (1976a, p. 27). Social disorganization is considered to be an accumulation of social dysfunctions (1976a, p. 37). More specifically, Merton identifies four sources of social disorganization (1976a, pp. 26, 27):

— conflicting interests and values;
— conflicting status and role obligations;
— faulty socialization;
— faulty social communication.

It is clear that in this model, there is a strong image of social groups as requiring a cultural structure and institutional structure that operate to damp down the inherent conflicts and divergences to at least an operable level. The model assumes widespread consensus, within which there is considerable, but not unlimited, room for dissensus. Social disorganization arises only when the normal coping mechanisms are overwhelmed. However, there is some room for innovation and long-term change, as his central image of social structure indicates:

> The key concept bridging the gap between statics and dynamics in functional theory is that of strain, tension, contradiction or discrepancy between the component elements of social and cultural structure. Such strains may be dysfunctional for the social system in its then existing form; they may also be instrumental in leading to changes in that system. In any case, they exert pressures for change. When social mechanisms for control are operating effectively, these strains are kept within such bounds to limit change of the social structure ([1968b, p. 176]).

This tension between routine and creative aspects of deviant behaviour is captured elsewhere in Merton's writings in the contrast between aberrants ("who have nothing new to propose and nothing old to restore, but seek only to satisfy their private interests or to express their private cravings" (1976a [1982a, p. 74]) and nonconformists ("who thrust towards a new morality or a promise to restore a morality held to have been put aside in social practice" 1976a [1982a, p. 74]).

Merton's work in both reference-group and role theory has attracted considerable commentary and discussion, although it is difficult to come to a rapid assessment of the fate of Merton's contributions to these concepts (on reference-group theory see especially the collection edited by Hyman and Singer (1968) and for sociological role theory see the discussions in Jackson (1972), and more recently by Handel (1979) and Turner (1985)). Both of these two related areas of work have been largely dominated by empiricist social psychologists or social interactionist sociologists. Much recent work in role-theory has become caught up in very detailed classificatory exercises in which an array of terms is fitted into an overarching 'role' framework (e.g. Biddle, 1979). Alternatively, role terms are used often loosely to guide sociographic descriptions of roles or of social processes affecting them. Within these wide or loose formulations the structural acuteness of the Mertonian approach becomes blunted or lost. However, several important contributions to structural role analysis were included in *The Idea of Social Structure* (Blau, 1975; Rose Coser, 1975) and a more recent discussion suggests the convergence, or rather the complementarity, between structural and interactionist views of roles (Turner, 1985). Indeed, one of the more important theoretical and research programmes influenced by a Mertonian framework has been Blau's more recent work on macro-structures (foreshadowed in Blau, 1975b).

5.6 SOCIAL CHARACTER

Personality or character structure is occasionally deployed as an intervening 'variable' between cultural and social structure on the one hand and social choices and social practices on the other. There are several places, in particular, where Merton includes a personality 'level of analysis': the bureaucratic personality (1968b, p. 259), leadership capacity (1968b, pp. 402, 404), eminent scientists (1973, pp. 458, 459), or even in the propensity to adopt a ritualistic mode of adaptation (1968b, p. 205).

But, as a sociologist Merton rightly shuns close attention to character structure. Whenever 'personality' is involved in explanation it is seen as both being shaped by social circumstances and in turn shaping patterns of behaviour (and especially in amplifying further social tendencies already in train).

Sociological analyses can often assume that personality is a 'random' variable, merely creating background noise in the explanatory system. Merton points out that, at least in some situations, the individuals' choice amongst alternatives is further narrowed by socially constructed personality characteristics.

Through repeated exposure and consistent choice, grooves of repeated information-handling are laid down, and this in turn becomes a further factor built into the ongoing situation and thus reinforcing the social structure. Character structure laid down during earlier socialization, especially during childhood, which varies by social strata, may be particularly influential in later social situations. Merton's early comments, in his essay on anomie, on the role of the family in socialization and especially the way in which the underlying structures of language and social perceptions are latently absorbed by the child are prescient ([1968b, pp. 212, 213]).

5.7   INTERACTION CONTEXTS

Although Merton has never accorded it systematic and explicit attention, an interest in the micro-sociology of interaction is a continual thread throughout his work. In further formulations of his anomie theory ([1968b, pp. 233–235]; 1964a, pp. 231–235), Merton makes it very clear that he considers that the interaction context plays a significant role either in amplifying or damping-down the vulnerability of individuals to anomic strain and their likelihood of converting this into deviant behaviour.

This same interest threads through other work: in particular the analysis of the network position of community influentials, the concomitant work on the dynamics of friendship links, studies of author–referee pairs, and the importance of social interaction if scientists are to sharpen their scientific ideas (1973, p. 347).

5.8   SOCIAL CHOICES

At the centre of the Mertonian analytical system is the action of individual people in making choices amongst structurally given alternatives. This component in the schema provides his 'model of man' (or social psychology or philosophical anthropology: cf. Wrong, 1961).

The actor is only partly socially determined in the Mertonian schema, and is conceptualized as having room to manoeuvre within structurally imposed constraints. The flesh-and-blood individual is also recognized as actively manning the positions in the social structure. By standing at the centre of often-diverse status-sets, the individual 'pulls together' the diverse strands and complexities of the social structure. In turn, the impulses and strains affecting an individual are structurally channelled through the lines of the social structure.

Despite the central place of the actor in Merton's system of theorizing, it has been a relatively unexplicated component of it. Nevertheless, we can draw on two discussions — the early treatment in the essay on "The unanticipated consequences of purposive social action" (1936b) and the more recent recapitulation by Stinchcombe (1975) which in turn has been confirmed by Merton (1976b, p. 124).

This early work was based on the analysis of the Chicago economist Frank Knight (1921) and is concerned to show how objective consequences can arise unbidden from purposive action. (The connection with Frank Knight seems to be an interesting one which is little explored: Knight not only translated Weber and continued an interest in this area, but also helped found the currently predominant "Chicago/Friedman" school of Economics. Does this hint at any underlying cognitive unity?) Purposive action is defined as ". . . 'conduct' as distinct from 'behaviour', that is, with action that involves motives and consequently a choice between alternatives" (1976b, p. 147). This is not to be assumed to be reducible to psychological reflexes, nor involving a clear-cut explicit purpose nor even involving a rational model. One of the major ways in which unanticipated consequences may arise is through limitations to the 'existing state of knowledge' on which social action is based. These limitations are barriers to the correct anticipating of consequences, and include (1936b [1976b, pp. 149–155]):

— ignorance (not only is knowledge of human affairs limited, but even more difficult is organizing means to achieve an aim);
— error (especially in applying knowledge to a particular situation);
— imperious immediacy of interest (a sharp focus on one set of consequences may exclude consideration of other consequences);
— basic values (consequences are not considered because of the overriding importance accorded the action by cultural values);
— self-defeating prediction (the very awareness of a social prediction may itself lead to action to put into effect behaviour that will negate the original aim of the social action).

Stinchcombe's rendition is generally similar. He depicts Merton's conceptualization of the core process as the:

choice between socially structured alternatives. . . [which] differs from the choice process of economic theory, in which the alternatives are conceived to have inherent utilities. It differs from the choice process of learning theory, in which the alternatives are conceived to emit reinforcing or extinguishing stimuli. It differs from both of these in that. . . the utility or reinforcement of a particular alternative choice is thought of as socially established, as part of the institutional order (Stinchcombe, 1975, p. 12; quoted approvingly by Merton, 1976b, p. 124).

A later passage in the same essay contrasts Merton's model of choice with symbolic interactionism ("the choice determined by definitions of the situation") and Parsonian theory ("choices about inherent value dilemmas determined by cultural values": Stinchcombe, 1975, p. 14). Criticizing symbolic interactionism, Stinchcombe points out that because of wider social frameworks which impinge on people they cannot define situations as they please (1975, p. 15). Criticizing Parsonian theory, Stinchcombe argues that value dilemmas are pitched at too general an analytical level for the theory to be able to show how they affect people's choices.

Other aspects of Merton's 'model of man' can be gleaned from other parts of his writings. A central point in Merton's 'model of man' is the importance of the cognitive element. This is particularly pointed up in his publicizing of the 'Thomas Theorem': "If men define situations as real, they are real in their consequences" (1948d [1968b, p. 475]). In his essay on functional analysis this interest echoes in phrases such as unanticipated and unintended consequences.

As several writers have noted (e.g. Taylor *et al.*, 1973), Merton departs from the biologically based 'model of man' in Durkheim's anomie theory, in which social structure must control the primitive urges. In fact, Merton is rather less concerned with this, and more with distancing himself from a Freudian intellectual embrace. However, this does not extend to his holding a 'rational' model. Merton has pointed out that his framework does not assume that people's choices are necessarily utilitarian or rational, but may incorporate less considered action, such as that associated with some forms of juvenile delinquency, but nevertheless still arising out of socially structured stresses (1968b, p. 232).

Rose Coser (1975, p. 239) has argued more aggressively that Merton holds a rather more active 'model of man':

Merton has stood Durkheim on his head; rather than have the individual confronted with ready-made social norms that are external, coming down in toto, so to speak, for Merton individuals have to find their own orientations among the multiple, incompatible, and contradictory norms.

I think that it may also be informative to consider the considerable emphasis on 'stress' and similar concepts at this point. Stress seems to me to be one category of an underlying variable that might be labelled something like 'experience of society' which shapes a person's orientation to society, and is likely to lead to behavioural consequences. Perhaps, the interest in stress suggests that the way individuals monitor their social experiences is central to social analysis.

In sum, Merton's 'model of man' is complex, but compatible both with social analysis and with a vision that men have a considerable degree of autonomy.

5.9 SOCIALLY EXPECTED DURATIONS

Merton's most recent work has been in the area of 'socially expected durations' (SEDs), which makes explicit a theme that has been implicit in, and has occurred from time to time throughout, his writings. In an early article with Sorokin (1937) the concept of 'social time' is reviewed, and in later work the differential social structuring of time is teased out. SEDs are:

> socially prescribed or collectively patterned expectations about temporal durations imbedded in social structures of various kinds: for example, the length of time that individuals are institutionally permitted to occupy particular statuses (such as an office in an organization or a membership in a group); assumed probable durations of diverse kinds of social relationships (such as friendship or a professional–client relation); and the patterned and therefore anticipated longevity of individual occupants of statuses, of groups and of organizations (1984a, pp. 265, 266).

There are at least two sociological implications of SEDs: at the individual level they affect behaviour and at the collective level they help link social structure and individual behaviour (Merton, 1984a; De Lellio, 1985).

It is rather more difficult to see where this theme works into Merton's overall framework. Time can be seen as a basic resource (1936a [1973]) or as a property of groups and organizations, and particularly status-sequences. It is also, I think, basic to the social frameworks within which people make their choices about action. As in cost–benefit analysis, so in decision-making different time-preferences lead to rather different decisions. Those in some social locations prefer instant gratification, while those in other social locations use their ability to postpone their requirements to stack up more in the way of long-term resources. In their choice of time-frame, individuals are not simply able to choose, but are required to fit in with multiple, collectively determined time-frames.

5.10 SOCIAL PRACTICES

Description of the behavioural pattern resulting from the choice amongst the structured options is always a carefully crafted part of a Mertonian analysis. To grasp how Merton tackles this aspect of his schema, reference will be made to several examples, and then the more general principles will be elicited from these examples.

In his essay on anomie, a typology of five individual 'modes of adaptation' is developed, which cover acceptance or rejection of present cultural goals on the one hand, and acceptance or rejection of present institutionalized means for achieving these goals on the other. In addition, a stance of rejection-and-substitution is provided for (1938b [1968b, p. 194]). Cross-tabulating orientation to cultural goals against orientation to institutional means generates a typology, in which each cell is then 'labelled' as a different 'mode of adaptation' (see Fig. 8). A brief description of each may

Type	Modes of adaptation	Culture goals	Institutionalized means
1	Conformity	+	+
2	Innovation	+	−
3	Ritualism	−	+
4	Retreatism	−	−
5	Rebellion	+	+

Fig. 8 — Modes of adaptation.

be needed to appreciate the typology:

— conformity (conformity to both cultural goals and institutionalized means is the most common — modal — form of behaviour, and that there be considerable recruitment to this mode is seen as necessary to maintain a stable society);
— innovation (in which "the individual has assimilated the cultural emphasis on the goal without equally internalizing the institutional norms governing ways and means for its attainment", a mode especially fostered in American society by the cultural stress on success being ostensibly available to all, irrespective of their social origins);
— ritualism (the abandonment or scaling down of aspirations in relation to the goal, accompanied by a focusing on the means);
— retreatism (involving the relinquishment of both goals and means and thus a 'dropping out' from mainstream society, the least frequent form);
— rebellion (where "the institutional system is regarded as the barrier to

legitimized goals" — new values are adduced and alternative means mobilized to seek to put these into effect).

A typology of ethnic prejudice has been developed (Merton, 1948c), which involves the cross-tabulating of attitudes to ethnic groups (prejudice v. non-prejudice) against behaviour towards them (discrimination v. non-discrimination). Both attitudes and behaviour are seen as related to the 'official creed' of egalitarianism. The typology yields four types of mix of prejudice and discrimination (see Fig. 9) (1948c [1976b, p. 192]).

Type	Attitude dimension	Behaviour dimension
1 All-weather liberal	+	+
2 Fair-weather liberal	+	−
3 Fair-weather illiberal	−	+
4 All-weather illiberal	−	−

Fig. 9 — Typology of ethnic prejudice and discrimination.

Although these two typologies are particularly explicit examples, similar (if unrecognized) typologies underlie other Mertonian analyses. For example, in his work on the behavioural patterns of scientists there lurks a typology which is built around the tension between the concern for recognition and concern for the advancement of scientific knowledge.

Several general methodological principles can be developed from these examples. One point is that the focus is on a whole complex of behaviour rather than on a simple dependent variable such as voting. Secondly, this complex of behaviour is conceptualized at an abstract level, so that it involves a general strategy of behaviour, which might subsume a wide variety of different tactics. Third, in order to capture much of this diversity of behaviour, Merton develops typologies that are based on logical distinctions around a few key principles. This is clearly an analytical device which greatly simplifies the empirical diversity and gradations of 'real life', and the analytical skill lies in first of all setting up the main underlying dimension in the schema of logical possibilities, followed by careful logic in then expanding the framework of categories. Finally, it should be noted that behavioural patterns include both what might otherwise be termed 'attitudes' on the one hand and 'behaviour' on the other.

The different terminologies which can be used in discussing this component of Merton's model create some difficulty. The term 'behavioural pattern' under-emphasizes the attitudinal aspect which is also central to Merton's conception. The term 'social practice' or, better, 'alternative social practices' may capture the meaning more appropriately (moreover, it is at least partly legitimated by Merton's own reference to 'practice' in his work on discrimination (1948c [1976b])).

Once set up, a typology may be useful in descriptive sociographies. For example, Merton suggests empirical research to determine the proportion of the four prejudice–discrimination types in various geographic areas and amongst different social classes, major associations and nationality groups (1976b, p. 210). However, the main purpose of the typology is to then model different explanations of the social structural sources that differentially shape individual's choice of one or other of the alternatives available to them.

5.11   FEEDBACK AND LEAKAGE LOOPS

Some of Merton's essays have examined mechanisms of social dynamics and change — in general unanticipated consequences and specifically the self-fulfilling prophecy, the self-defeating or suicidal prophecy, and latent and manifest functions. This part of the schema is concerned with how the social practices resulting from social choices fold back to affect structures. The examples that bring this out include the way in which the practice of publishing (rather than non-publishing) then leads to the continuance of journals, and the way in which the practice of voting for a particular political party (rather than non-voting or voting for another party) will more likely result in the persistence of that political organization. Thus contributors and voters not only choose amongst options, but by making a particular choice they help to keep open the possibility of that option continuing to be available. This element of the overall model has already been presaged in the discussion of the conflict between alternative structures in Chapter 4 where it was noted that it is central to Stinchcombe's (1968) discussion of the causal imagery of functional analysis. It has also been adopted by sociologists such as Boudon (1981) as a framework for the tracing of 'perverse effects' at the aggregate level, that flow from individual decisions. (Note that this point also relates to the discussion about the relationship between the institutional and 'pre-institutional' levels of behaviour above.)

Although Merton has been particularly interested in these feedback mechanisms, he has not published work on their operation in detail. However, some of the examples he deploys in drawing attention to their operation are widely regarded as classic contributions. He defines a self-fulfilling prophecy as "a false definition of the situation evoking a new behaviour which makes the orginally false conception come true" (1948d [1968b, p. 477]). The examples he offers include the collapse of banks under 'runs' and the way in which people in minority groups have, in the past at least, not been allowed access to institutions and then damned because they pursued alternatives. The suicidal prophecy involves changing the course of behaviour such that the prophecy fails to be brought about. Merton is careful to point out that there are social mechanisms that can intervene in such vicious cycles and that institutional controls are often able to quell rumours and panics that feed at the informal interactional level of operation.

In addition to the feedback effects specified by Merton, Stinchcombe and Boudon there is another class of 'social practice effects' on structure that can be designated as 'leakage effects'. This is where social practices affect the development of 'neighbouring' structures other than those which generated the behaviour patterns in the first place. The obvious example of this is Merton's hypothesis that the Puritan impulse may have led to the increased pursuit of scientific knowledge. Leakage effects are not randomly sprayed around from their source, but are contained by the status-sets that people are simultaneously placed within. Often, however, this leakage effect will be unanticipated and unintended by the actors involved. It is a consequence of the way social structures are complexly organized.

The most obvious way in which consequences affect institutions is through building or collapsing the social support for a particular institution over against its rivals — the structural alternatives. However, the relationship may be more varied than this. For example, as a result of scientists' productivity, scientific work may accumulate into massive flows of articles. The resultant growth may in turn have effects on individual behaviour (e.g. the types of literature-searching practices needed to cope with the volume available).

5.12 SUMMARY

Having sketched out Merton's multi-layered analytical account, it is important to show how this is then 'set in motion' or made to 'work'. Merton places much emphasis on abjuring mere typologies, and requires that theoretical work posit 'causal' connections (see his comments reported in Chapter 3). This means that any full-blown Mertonian analysis must involve each of the components sketched out above. At this point we can again draw on some of the discussion presented by Stinchcombe.

At the centre of the schema is some pattern of choices faced by human actors, and this is seen as constrained and often routinized in continually repeated patterns, but still with a solid spark of 'free will'. However, the act of choice is the result of a variety of sources — both psychological and sociological. Merton's sociological analytical apparatus focuses on the structuring of choices and motivation, so that the actor plays a subordinate role in the system.

Instead, Merton's analytical schema locates the seat of energy in the cultural structure, but as mediated, reinforced or dampened by the social structure. It is their joint effect that shapes the range of choice for individuals. While the cultural structure provides the knowledge and values which circumscribe and motivate social action, these are variously effected by social structure, not least through differential exposure to the cultural structure. At the centre of all Merton's analyses are social structural features, which more specifically shape social practices, and which in turn differentially affect the development of culture and also feedback to gradually reshape the social structure itself.

It is difficult to evoke the imagery behind Merton's schema, although its explanatory bite is largely lost if we cannot conjure up a metaphor. Classic functionalism used the biological analogy of a homeostatic system, such as the blood circulation system of a body, in which any perturbation is fairly quickly restored back to equilibrium through the mechanisms which maintain body temperature. The more advanced versions of Parsons's thought might be likened somewhat to a very complicated energy-exchange motor system (a very sophisticated car engine) in which a variety of fuels circulate and can be in part transmogrified into each other although they are in part quite compartmentalized. Lukes has pointed out that in Durkheim's writing much is made of imagery drawn from thermodynamics and electricity (1973, p. 35). The imagery behind Merton's approach is different, but equally complicated.

It seems to me that Merton's structural analysis might be imagined as rather like a water-skier being towed behind at least two speed-boats, but where there is an intermediate structure of a variety of pulleys, levers and tubular steel frames which both amplify, damp down and certainly complicate the pull from the boats to the skier. The skier has some, albeit limited, control over the boats — if only the requirement that the boats must stop to pick up the skier should he or she fall. This image conveys the idea of the distant and multidirectional pulling-power of the cultural structure, and of the limited but significant role of the actor in maintaining the balancing act of resolving in their performance some of the conflicting demands upon them. It also conveys an appropriate image of both the pressure towards conformity in behaviour as it is continuously enacted, but also the precariousness of this performance and the continual pressures to diverge into alternative paths. A difficulty with this imagery is that it is not too easy to fit in the typology of choices, although it is possible to glimpse some possibilities.

This imagery has several attractive features (compare the account given in Stinchcombe, 1975, pp. 26–31). The scale at which the analysis is cast 'brings men in' (to use Homans's phrase), but also shows how their behaviour is socially shaped. There is a focus on regularity in human affairs but also attention to ambivalence, deviance and reaction, and the vulnerability of the accepted social order to change. Social structure is portrayed as being real in its effects, but it is seen as permeable rather than reified. Private troubles and joys are linked to structure but structure is shown to grow out of individual behaviour in a nice interplay of the objective and subjective. The mix of handling the ordinary and the exotic, the obvious and the mysterious is nicely grasped: Merton urges attention to the unobvious hidden side of the social which only sociologists can reveal, but he also attempts to confront the commonplace by showing the limitations of commonsense assumptions. Nevertheless the mundane is built into his sociology as much as the newly revealed. While the Mertonian system is clearly able to handle variety in human behaviour, its ability to explain change and its handling of power need closer examination.

In Stinchcombe's exegesis the feedback-looping is given a prominent place. But, as in Merton's work, examples of changing structures are not prominent, despite the central point in functional analysis that structural equivalents might be expected to 'come in' once a particular structure is seen to be failing, and despite his concern that long-term viability of any social structure is dependent on mechanisms that induce change. Merton also clearly feels that his approach has a weak spot in this area and discusses this in later reflections on his essay on "Social Structure and Anomie":

Unless systematic consideration is given to the degree of support of particular 'institutions' by specific groups, we shall overlook the important place of power in society. To speak of 'legitimate power' or authority is often to use an elliptical and misleading phrase. Power may be legitimized for some without being legitimized for all groups in a society. It may, therefore, be misleading to describe non-conformity with particular institutions merely as deviant behaviour; it may represent the beginning of a near alternative pattern, with its own distinctive claims to moral validity (1968b, p. 176).

An interest in the role of power in creating or confounding change is included within his discussion of the postulate of universal functionalism.

Far more useful [than this postulate, he suggests] would seem the provisional assumption that persisting cultural forms have a *net balance of functional consequences* [Merton's emphasis] either for the society considered as a unit or for subgroups sufficiently powerful to retain these forms intact, *by means of direct coercion or indirect persuasion* [my emphasis] (Merton, 1968b, p. 86).

Beneath the intricate but bland Mertonian facade there lurks a flavour of *realpolitik* that is seemingly suppressed elsewhere! It is through such mechanisms that the Mertonian analytical system is able to explain how the structure is itself able to induce structural changes, whereas the Parsonian system seems only to react to external changes. Merton briefly endorses the approach taken by Stinchcombe that change, even revolutionary change, can be broken down in repeated cycles of structurally induced changes, provided that the time frame can be frozen sufficiently (Merton, 1976b). In joint work with Lazarsfeld, Merton had already developed a similar model of the process of development of a friendship (Merton and Lazarsfeld, 1954). At several points, he suggests that there is something of a 'social learning' process as the social structure develops an increasing ability to handle certain endemic difficulties (for example in handling stresses in status-and-role structures). However, Merton is more often than not taken with the irony that change or conflict can feedback onto social order, as expressed in his almost triumphant citation of the Simmel–Ross theory of conflict:

a society . . . which is riven by a dozen . . . [conflicts] along lines running in every direction, may actually be in less danger of being torn with violence or falling to pieces than one split along just one line. For each new cleavage contributes to narrow the cross clefts, so that one might say that society is sewn together by its inner conflicts (Merton, 1961b [1973, p. 68] citing Ross).

However, these areas of power and change remain a seemingly potential explanatory aspect of his system that has not been sufficiently developed, because analysis has not been focused on them. Because of this limited attention Merton's sociology is rather too trapped in the deficiencies which are held to afflict all Durkheimian-derived sociologies.

5.13   REVIEW

I shall conclude this discussion of Merton's underlying analytical apparatus by attempting to evaluate the validity of his conception compared to

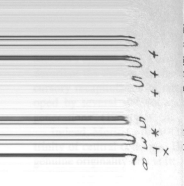

is time-period, by reviewing criticisms of it,
ount of influence on Merton. How original is
gy? Sorokin, with his charming insouciance
nce-groups as "a somewhat fragmented and
e adequate theories of social groups devel-
[unnamed!] of the preceding and present

in the general 'culture, society, personality'
owever, I feel that his schema does possess

rnal components of these three broad areas
the lattice-work of statuses and roles which
;
ial nature and 'relative autonomy' of each
major component, and to specify some of the mechanisms through
which each interacts with the other (for example, in suggesting that
pressure towards deviant behaviour is generated by the mismatch
between cultural and social structure);
— links these three general 'explanatory' concepts to behavioural patterns
or social practices (which include the feedback loop of reproduction or
change in the structures generating the pattern), so that Merton always
focuses on something to explain, rather than merely providing reified
descriptive categories.

In sum, Merton took the 'culture, society, personality' schema, differen-
tiated more finely within it, connected it up and set it to work on explaining
behaviour. As with most other creative activities (Koestler, 1973; Merton,
1965) the various materials for the extension of past work were at hand. But
they needed to be activated.

Merton was an avowed functional analyst for most of his academic life
(during the late 1940s through to the early 1970s), and before this operated
with a simplified and truncated version of this approach. In the mid-1970s
he partially recanted, but did not clearly enunciate what was involved in the
non-Parsonian structural 'variant' he now was prepared to accept, or clarify
his attitude to his earlier work. In this book, I have argued that under the
cover of this functional framework, Merton in fact largely deployed a
structuralist approach, in which behavioural outcomes are tied to structural
sources. The top-layer of Merton's functional analysis has unfortunately
and confusedly distracted attention from the rather more important underlying structural analysis.

It is possible to revisit criticisms of his earlier work to show that they do not undermine his structural analyses. The difficulty with the functional mode of interpretation arose when Merton attempted to extend his earlier model of unanticipated consequences, to deal with the particular — but sociologically strategic — subclass of unanticipated consequences that affect the continuance of social institutions. The difficulty with explanations couched in these terms is that they can appear to 'explain' a social institution, or the continued existence of a social institution, in terms of its consequences. This not only unnecessarily reifies social structure, but appears to commit the aggregative fallacy of according social aggregates with intentionality and understanding. Only actors can act, although they may act in some part with a concern about the maintenance of social structure.

Despite these philosophical difficulties, using the language of functions may continue to have a useful heuristic purpose in alerting social analysts to interlocking connections between diverse social phenomena, provided that at least in principle a translation into individual-level terms is possible. This is a version of the doctrine of 'methodological individualism'.

Merton's 'functional interpretations' did not fall into the traps of 'functional explanations', although perhaps he may not have clearly enough distanced himself from the latter. In each of his functional analyses, it is possible for it to be converted into such terms by showing that continuance or change in institutional patterns result from individual consequences — whether intended or not.

The challenge then becomes to show that Merton's classic examples of functional analysis can be reconstructed according to the above rule (i.e. recasting as a causal analysis and in terms of 'methodological individualism'). Merton has been criticized by several commentators (e.g. Matza, 1969, pp. 59, 60) for breaching his own methodological strictures by arguing that the "the functional deficiencies of the official structure generated an alternative unofficial structure to fulfill existing needs somewhat more effectively" (1968b, p. 127). That is, the continuity of the political machine proves its functionality. However, although such an interpretation of Merton's rather casual functional analysis of political machines can be made, a rather more careful reading of the complete passage indicates that:

— Merton establishes that there is a 'need' for services, such as those supplied by a political machine;
— Merton argues that political machines contrive to operate in the face of some opposition from decent citizens, and competition from alternative sources of supply for those services.

alternative structures. Individual involvement in such patterns strongly tends to be self-reinforcing.

Some critics have noted that Merton's conception of consequences involves them being (un)anticipated or (un)intended or both. Merton's preference for the term (un)anticipation over (un)intention may be in line with his more general theme of cognition, information etc. (as Giddens, (1984), has pointed up). It seems to me, however, that 'intention' is preferable on at least two grounds:

— intention subsumes anticipation (or knowledge) — "one cannot intend something to happen without anticipating that it might happen" (Giddens, 1984, p. 38);
— motivation is rather more at issue than knowledge.

Another interesting critical point that has emerged is Giddens's useful observation that Merton's concern with the self-fulfilling/negating aspects of predictions underlines a dramatic difference in the operation of social as opposed to natural laws.

Even if the latent structure of Merton's analytical apparatus is not readily apparent, aspects of his approach have already attracted criticism. Sometimes it is difficult to judge the degree of impact of such criticism, especially when some seems ignorant and other points are contradicted. Some areas of criticism have already been mentioned in relevant sections above; more specific criticism will be included in the next chapter, while the last two chapters develop a more systematic overall critical perspective.

Finally, it is now possible to revisit the earlier account of the sources drawn upon by Merton in constructing the analytical apparatus he deployed in substantive studies, although it is not appropriate here to develop a full-scale accounting. It should suffice to point to the diversity of theoretical sources — Chicago social theory (especially the Thomas theorem), social anthropology, as well as the range of European social theorists that other accounts indicate — Marx, Durkheim, Simmel, Weber and Freud (compare the account in Stinchcombe, 1975, p. 14). But the Mertonian model cannot be reduced to any of these, and it clearly contains 'emergent properties' in its selection and presentation.

6.1 INTRODUCTION

In this chapter, I examine Merton's contributions in the two main substantive areas in which he wrote, in order to see what light these shed on his more general model, as outlined in Chapter 5. One test of the correctness of my conceptualization of Merton's general sociological structures is to find them embedded in his more substantive work. In addition, it might be expected that a close examination of more substantive work might reveal additional angles on his more general approaches. It might also be expected, that critics will obtain more leverage on Merton's substantive, rather than his general statements, and that drawing on these will more clearly reveal deficiencies and limitations. Besides their possible contribution to deepening understanding of his general sociology, it is important to examine these substantive contributions in their own right, as much of Merton's impact on sociology has been through his work in particular specialities.

It is not without significance that Merton has contributed to two areas of sociology which have at various times been central to the overall development of sociology, as crucial issues have been most visibly raised and fought over in these areas. In the late 1960s and through the 1970s, the area of sociology in which viewpoints (such as the labelling perspective) broadly deriving from a symbolic interactionist stance were most exercised was the sociology of deviance. This was followed by arguments about deviance derived from a radical, Marxian perspective. Together they placed the sociology of deviance as an area which was the leading edge of theoretical development and debate in sociology.

About a decade later the sociology of science performed a somewhat similar role, although one less central to the whole of sociology. Fuelled by issues imported from the adjacent areas of philosophy and the history of science, many of the major theoretical debates affecting sociology as a whole have been played out within the sociology of science in a particularly intense form.

This has meant that in both these substantive areas Merton's ideas have been addressed rather more closely than might otherwise have occurred.

6.2   MERTON'S CONTRIBUTIONS TO SOCIOLOGY OF DEVIANCE

Compared to the volume and steady progression of material Merton produced in the sociology of science and its related context of the sociology of knowledge, his contributions to the sociology of deviance are sparse, episodic and focused. Indeed, it consists of one article published in the late 1930s, reworked in the late 1940s, together with a few elaborations and comments added in the late 1950s and early 1960s. The almost full weight of his impact is borne by this one early article, as his later extensions very usefully round out the perspective, but really add little to the main structure of the argument. It should be noted that Merton draws attention to the extended version by referring to it as 'anomie-and-opportunity-structure' theory. Cole (1975, p. 185) suggests:

> It would be an error to see the theory of SSOA as a single paper. The theory is in fact a research program which Merton developed over a thirty-year period. If one compares the initial 1938 paper with a more recent statement such as the Merton essay in the Clinard collection, one can easily see that the theory has been added to and modified. It has been a dynamic rather than a static theory, developing in response to its environment.

(However, having said this, Cole then undermines his own argument by contenting himself with one version.)

Perhaps what is most surprising is that although 'Social Structure and Anomie' is arguably the most cited article in sociology, its empirical backing is sketchy, and has never been flanked by empirical work from Merton himself (although he proposed an extensive 'design of inquiry' in 1964: 1964a).

Merton's theory concerns the explanation of different rates of deviance by the differential location of people within a particular 'opportunity structure'. Because of socially structured gaps between aspirations (shared goals) and actual achievement (access to the social means for achieving those goals), the power of the dominant social norms (which operationalize

— the extent to which money is fetishized as a sign of success, and
— the way in which the dominant ideology nicely deflects any criticism of
  the social structure back into blaming the unsuccessful victims.

Differential rates of deviance between people in different social locations
are seen to be the results of different motivations and access to means, with
these in turn being generated by these locations. The opportunity structure
consists in several alternative social positions which vary in terms of their
access to the means for achieving these goals. These positions are organized
in three groupings — conforming, aberrant and nonconforming — which in
detail involves (as already discussed in Chapter 5):

— conformists (accepting both goals and means)
— innovators (accepting the goal but rejecting the means)
— ritualists (rejecting the goal but continuing adherence to the means)
— retreatists (rejecting both goals and means)
— rebels (rejecting both goals and means and substituting new versions of
  both).

Rebels are clearly separated from the other forms of deviant behaviour (as
nonconforming rather than aberrant). Using this framework, Merton then
is able to portray many Americans as plodding conformists, hollow ritualists, desolate retreatists, desperate innovators or creative rebels.

A further development of the theory asserts linkages between particular
social strata and one or other of the five likely outcomes. Only two linkages

are indicated: ritualism is seen as more frequent amongst the lower-middle class, whereas innovation is seen as more frequent amongst the working class.

The provenance of Merton's interest in deviance is largely unknown. Later (1964a), Merton is content to laconically observe that "It was in this local climate of sociological theory, induced by Sorokin and Parsons, that I found myself focusing on the theoretical problems of the master sources of anomie. . ." (p. 215). The provenance of the basic idea involved is rather more obvious. As Cole points out (1975, p. 187), that although "perhaps the most significant influence on Merton's work was Durkheim's development of the concept of anomie", yet this source is only briefly mentioned, and in the original article the single, forlorn reference to Durkheim cites *The Rules of Sociological Method* rather than the more obviously related *Suicide*. As Merton makes clear (1964a, pp213,214) this idea is so well known that it hardly needed detailed citation.

There have been several major extensions and reformulations of Merton's anomie theory: Talcott Parsons (1951) uses three variables to develop a typology of eight types of deviant behaviour, and generalizes deviance beyond that arising from the stress generated when cultural goals do not mesh with means. Dubin (1959) also attempts to extend Merton's typology of types of deviant, in his case by adding a variable of 'attitude to norms' between goals and means, and then by distinguishing between behavioural and value innovation and ritualism.

Cloward (1959) suggests extending the concept of opportunity-structure by adding to Merton's variable of 'access to legitimate means', a further variable of 'access to illegitimate means' and points out that the access to learning and opportunity components of either sort of means is socially structured. Cloward's extension suggests that "different strata provide varying opportunities for the acquisition of deviant roles, largely through access to deviant subcultures and the opportunity for carrying out such deviant social roles once they have been acquired" (as summarized by Clinard, 1964, p. 27). Cloward and Ohlin (1960) later developed this further in studying the formation of delinquent subcultures. Depending on whether the social surrounds of a group are integrated or not: either criminal, conflict or retreatist group responses are likely. 'Retreatist' gangs are seen as 'double failures' — unsuccessful in employing either legitimate or illegitimate means to success. With this extension of Merton's framework, Cloward and Ohlin claim to be linking anomie theory to the earlier idea of E. H. Sutherland that deviance is spread through cultural transmission and differential association.

Cohen (1959), while critical of much of Merton's framework, seeks to add a more explicit interactionist aspect, and to bring in reference-group

texts) and suggest too abrupt a switch from strain to deviancy (whereas deviance may more often be built up gradually within an interactional framework);

(2) Many deviant acts arise out of role expectations rather than disjunctions between goals and means;

(3) Since they are so linked, the analytical separation of cultural goals and social means may be too artificial;

(4) Given the pluralist nature of complex modern societies it may be difficult to identify a set of universal cultural goals shared by all;

(5) The societal conditions generating anomie may be limited to societies stressing achieved rather than ascribed statuses;

(6) It is possible that the empirical foundations are incorrect, given methodological difficulties with official data on deviance;

(7) It is not explained why most of the lower class is prepared to conform;

(8) Support for the cultural goals may not be uniform over all social classes;

(9) Societal reaction in actively defining deviance is ignored;

(10) The social conditions influencing different forms of adaptation — especially retreatism — are not specified.

Several of these points seem relatively unimportant, and some seem, to me, to be adequately covered in at least the later versions of the theory, which include elements of the associational and deviant-opportunity-structure approaches.

However, at least two empirical areas of criticism are important. There is some evidence that while there is widespread sharing of important social goals — such as the value of educational credentials — that there are sharp class differentials (see Merton, 1968b, pp. 224–228; Thio, 1975). The problem is whether to read the evidence as supporting the view of consensus or dissensus in terms of overarching goals (such as the culturally induced drive for material success). This is clearly a complex question in which the type of goals involved (e.g. their degree of abstractness), the level of support and the necessary methodology to research this are all problematic. But, this question is really most affected by alternative theoretical stances. Those working out from an 'interpretative' position are unlikely to perceive cultural uniformities, whereas few Marxists are likely to disagree with a view that capitalist societies are dominated by an ideological hegemony that covers a wide range of materialistic cultural goals including individual success motives. From a Marxist viewpoint this hegemony is in large part imposed, and works to the benefit of the 'ruling classes', but nevertheless has deep impacts on people from all classes.

The second crucial question is the extent to which there are class differentials in deviance. Thio (1975) has provided the sharpest critique, and suggests that by continuing to use what he regards as class-biased data, Merton is stigmatizing the lower class. Thio draws an analogy with the fierce controversy over the apparent social class distribution of intelligence. Instead, he suggests deviance may be more prevalent amongst the upper class. However, Matza (1969, p. 99) suggests that if anything, the official statistics point to the high prevalence of official deviance amongst the *lumpenproleteriat* rather than throughout the working-class as a whole, and he castigates the anomie theorists for their lack of attention to relevant empirical data (especially on patterns of working-class mobility).

A theoretical problem remains about the relationship between Mertonian anomie theory and Durkheim's analysis of anomie and also its relationship to Marx's analysis of alienation (which several scholars have attended to: Horton, 1964; Taylor, 1971; Taylor *et al.*, 1973; Fenton, 1983). Thio argues that Durkheim developed two conceptions of anomie (see also the discussion in Simon and Gagnon (1976)):

— as a sudden break in life events;
— as a chronic condition generated by highly developed divisions-of-labour.

In both types of anomie, the upper classes are more likely to be affected than the lower class.

Poverty protects against (anomie) because it is a restraint in itself.

nor the inegalitarian social structure are explained:

> It is as though individuals in society are playing a gigantic fruit machine, but the machine is rigged and only some players are consistently rewarded. The deprived ones then either resort to using foreign coins or magnets to increase their chances of winning (innovation) or play on mindlessly (ritualism), give up the game (retreatism) or propose a new game altogether (rebellion). But in the analysis nobody appeared to ask who put the machine there in the first place and who takes the profits. Criticism of the game is confined to changing the pay-out sequences so that the deprived can get a better deal (Taylor, 1971, p. 148).

It is interesting, from the perspective argued in this book, to note that the 'anomie' theory of deviance is seldom labelled as a functional theory. For example, in the Clinard collection 'function' does not seem to be used except in the strict sense of the functional consequences of deviance, and is not included in the index. This unconcern to locate the anomie theory under a broader theoretical umbrella such as 'functional analysis' seems supportive of my argument (in Chapter 5) about the general role of Merton's theories.

There is actually some explicit attention to a functional analysis of deviance within Merton's theory of deviance. In the main version of his essay, Merton notes, amongst other limitations, that his essay "has only briefly considered the social functions fulfilled by deviant behaviour " (1968b, p. 214) which is an interesting indication that Merton saw his analysis as mainly other than a functional one. However, in the introduction to the reprint of this essay in *Social Theory and Social Structure* Merton reworks the framework of his anomie theory to stress that it involves an analytical concern with social and cultural change (1968b, p. 176).

> The key concept bridging the gap between statics and dynamics in functional theory is that of strain, tension, contradiction or discrepancy between the component elements of social and cultural structure. Such strains may be dysfunctional for the social system in its then existing form; they may also be instrumental in leading to changes in that system.

It is clearly possible to develop a functional analysis of non-conformity which spells out its consequences for wider social systems, and Merton is alert to the need to distinguish short-term and long-term effects of deviance.

However, the main overwhelming thrust of anomie theory is clearly structural and causal: social structure causes differential behaviour, mediated by 'strain'. As the anomie theory formulation is refracted widely throughout other parts of Merton's work, the importance of this essentially 'structural' formulation is particularly strategic.

6.3   MERTON'S CONTRIBUTIONS TO SOCIOLOGY OF SCIENCE

Although Storer (1973, p. xi) is unnecessarily reluctant to accord Merton the title of the founding father of the sociology of science, it is clear that the title is deserved. Merton's work in this area spans fifty years, divided into an early series of contributions up to the mid-1940s which established a general perspective on science as an historically developing social institution, subject to influences from other institutions, and a later series of contributions from the late 1950s to the mid-1970s which include more contemporary empirical investigations and a theoretical model of the 'internal' workings of science. Alongside his writing on science have been continuing interests in the sociology of knowledge and the sociology of social science, but these will be attended to only where necessary to understand his sociology of natural science. My account will largely follow that provided by Storer (1973) but with an added focus on points salient to my purposes.

Merton's interest in sociology of science seems to have developed in a Harvard intellectual atmosphere in which a variety of scholars (including E. F. Gay, economic historian; George Sarton, historian of science; L. J. Henderson, biochemist, historian of science and social systems analyst;

Merton is at pains to point out that the two thrusts of argument are held together with an overall concern to analyse the *inter*dependence between science as a social institution and other areas of society. The first line of argument was an outrageous hypothesis garnered from Weber (at first diffusely and eventually supported by the one sentence Weber wrote on this) that not only was the impetus to the development of science generated from outside scholarly institutions but was in fact located in the religious sphere — that erstwhile enemy of science. Moreover, within the religious spectrum of the time, Merton sought to show that it was from the otherwise unlikely dour and theologically encumbered Puritan/Pietist sects that this impetus had specifically sprung. The second line of analysis is rather more straightforward, although of equal high sociological relevance: it is an attempt to empirically specify the extent to which Marxian analyses of the dependence of science on dominant social and economic interests seemed to be correct (in fact, Merton was able to document a major if not completely hegemonic impact).

By the late 1930s, Merton began to add to his analyses of the impacts of non-science institutions on scientific work and scientists' motivation, an appreciation of science as a social institution in its own right. This began, as part of an essay reacting to the threatening loss of autonomy of German science in the Nazi era, by attempting to analyse the cultural conditions which support scientific work (1938c). In this analysis it was pointed out that the norms stressing the purity of science have as a functional consequence the furnishing of an ideological defence useful in the protection of science from the incursion of other interests, although this studied indifference to other institutional areas can also breed negative reaction against science because of the economic and social consequences of scientific inventions. Further, another value of science — 'organized scepticism' — can become a social threat when directed at values held in other institutional spheres. In 1942 this conceptualization of science as a social institution was extended with a fuller statement of the 'ethos of science' — the *moral norms* of universalism, communism, organized scepticism and disinterestedness that were seen to shape the social practice of science, alongside such socially supported *technical norms* as the need to provide both adequate, valid and reliable empirical evidence and the need for logical consistency. These norms were seen to be the social integument which allowed the implementation of the technical methods needed to achieve the institutional goal of the extension of certified knowledge. With this analysis, Merton had succeeded in shifting his attention from the external social conditions which influence the development of science, to an analysis of the internal structure of science. Storer argues that this conceptualization of science was theoretically significant, although not widely recognized as such at the time, and that it informed Merton's later theoretical work on the social organization of science.

From the mid-1930s Merton was also concerned to establish the foundations of a systematic sociology of science by securing the properly couched problematics of the area and by attention to methodology: thus his 1938 essay on 'science and the social order' raises questions on a particularly sociological plane, while (as Storer notes, 1973, xviii) '. . . his early (1937) paper with Sorokin, "The Course of Arabian Intellectual Development, 700–1300 A.D." is subtitled "A Study in Method" '.

In 1952, during the interlude between his early and late periods of work in the sociology of science, Merton wrote a brief foreword to the book on Science written by his student Bernard Barber (the only student over an 18-year period he had been able to recruit into the sociology of science). This foreword notes some recent interest in sociology of science, rues that there has not been more, and predicts that further attention to this area would only occur once science had been widely defined as a social problem.

Merton's return to an interest in sociology of science was launched through the highly visible forum of his 1957 Presidential Address to the American Sociological Society. This address involved a reconceptualization of the social structure of science aroused by a continued interest in the phenomena of multiple discovery, priority disputes and the commemorative use of eponymy in science. Central to this:

". . . was the conceptualization that the institutionally reinforced drive for professional recognition, acquired almost exclusively in return for

somewhat undermined by petty squabbles over priority and desire for the immortality of recognition.

While many scientists work quietly at assigned puzzles, the motivation for intense scientific activity is the reward of recognition which flows from having been the first to make a discovery. The discovery becomes an 'intellectual property' from which a 'symbolic rent' can be derived in the form of prestige. The more significant the advance, the higher the prestige accorded the discoverer, and therefore with such high stakes, the more potent the likelihood of priority disputes.

A significant implication of this approach is that it sets up science as a separate social institution, with its own internal mechanism of peer recognition, ensuring that scientists are motivated to distance their activities from those fitting within other institutional spheres. (For example, recognition can be accorded by peers, not the general public.)

This theoretical framework also allows Merton to identify various deviances likely to arise within the scientific community as a result of particular discontinuities between the cultural and social structures of science.

Having established this basic framework for analysing science, Merton was then able to raise and examine an array of subsequent questions, including:

— variation over time in the conditions under which scientific competition becomes intensified;
— the role of 'geniuses' in science as opposed to the total social determination of ideas ("It was precisely the great scientists, [Merton] points out, who prove to be most capable of exploiting the current state of the

art — they are involved in many more multiples than others — so that the two theoretical perspectives actually complement each other": (Storer in Merton, 1973, p. 284);
— different theoretical and policy implications of the phenomenon of multiple discoveries;
— the stress and inner conflict induced in scientists by the complexities and trade-offs involved within the normative structure of science;
— the consequences for the operation of science of the accumulation of recognition by the scientific elite;
— an examination of the actual working of the system of evaluating the quality of scientific work, through the refereeing system and other structural modes of organized scepticism;
— the consequences for scientific activity of differences in the organization of knowledge in a discipline (its degree of codification);
— the impact of demographic structure (age, and in the work of Jonathan Cole, 1979, gender) on the social organization of science.

The general thrust of this rapid exploitation of his own paradigm has been to explore further the various components of the internal structure of science in order to detail its workings. This has involved progressively examining each of a set of different axes of differentiation (gender, age, etc.) within science and different parts of the institutional complex of science in order to build up a more complete picture.

This set of studies has been particularly facilitated through the Columbia University Programme in the Sociology of Science, supported by the National Science Foundation. Collaborative work has also meant that, while these essays retain the Mertonian stamp of theoretical argument coupled with an historically rich scatter of illustration, they also include extensive systematic empirical research support.

Merton summarizes his own later work in the sociology of science as follows:

"It was along such lines [i.e. the interaction between social and intellectual influences internal and external to the institution of science] that, during the later 1940s and intermittently in the next decade, I continued my work on problems of the normative structure of science and turned to processes involved in its social organization. Attention was first centred on the process of social and cognitive competition in what Michael Polanyi called 'the scientific community' Starting in the middle 1950s, this plan of work led to further inquiry into patterns of competition among scientists, the reward structure of science as related

ledge and the communication networks (the 'invisible colleges') through which scientists work;
— Polanyi's essays on the 'republic of science';
— Eugene Garfield's development of citation indexes for science (and later for social science and the humanities — in which the linkages between scientific papers can be traced).

American work in the sociology of science, including the Columbia University Programme, drew on several of these developments, while being guided theoretically and practically by Merton. The Mertonian school was able to achieve a rapid breakthrough by harnessing the quantitative analyses of productivity, and especially the quality of scientific production using citation indices, fitting them into models of stages of scientific growth extended from Price. Having established measures of the meritocratic order of scientists, the American sociologists of science then examined whether science, and especially its reward systems, operate in the 'objective' interests of science as a whole. Against this meritocratic model, they have sought to examine whether particularistic characteristics, such as age, gender or the academic institution scientists are based in, intrude into the production of scientific knowledge. Thus, examination of the stratificational system of science is central to the Mertonian programme in the sociology of science. In general, this programme of investigation has found that the actual operation of science cleaves fairly closely, but with some jarring, to this meritocratic model. In the work of the Mertonians, this then becomes explained in terms of a 'functional' model of stratification, in which the internal stratificational order (which they usually express as three strata of scientists of the first, second or third order) is seen as more-or-less correctly mirroring the distribution of talent, and thus being functional for the ongoing progress of science.

Alongside this main focus on the stratificational system of science has been a continued, but minor, interest in the analysis of the cultural goals of science. But if the empirical attention paid to this is slender, its theoretical weight is great. For the universalistic and other norms of science are invoked to explain its more-or-less universalistic mode of operation.

However, the status of these norms in the Mertonian account is problematic: as it is not clear whether they are seen as 'necessary' for the advance of science (or even 'deduced' from an analysis of the requirements of science) or whether they have a causal force in their own right (see Gieryn, 1982, p. 295; Kuhn, 1977, p. xxii). It seems more than likely that the 'moral norms' of science have a multiple effect as *both* ideology and driving force. In the most recent Mertonian work on this topic, Zuckerman (1978) shows that these general norms are complexly built) into the instutional structure of science.

A further line of interpretation has been marginal to the mainstream work of the Mertonian empirical research programme, although of very considerable theoretical importance. Hagstrom (1965) in an intensive and then extensive analysis of competition and concern for priority in science and Gaston (1970) looking at these topics in relation to English scientists developed Merton's interest in priority-disputes as strategic research-sites for understanding the character of intellectual property in science. Both Hagstrom, and later Storer (1966) developed a social psychological 'exchange' theory of scientific behaviour from this aspect of Merton's work. This involved conceptualizing science as an institutional area in which the rewards granted scientists were tightly linked to the provision of valued contributions to science.

Both early and later phases of Merton's work in the sociology of science have generated controversies. Merton's work on the historical flowering of science in the seventeenth century has lead to a complicated and vigorous debate within the history and historical sociology of science. This long debate has been marred by much misunderstanding arising over the specification of the concepts and terms involved (see Abraham, 1983) and has also involved much inch-by-inch trench warfare. Since the significance of the debate is very largely about matters of fact rather than forms of explanation, a detailed tour of the distant site over which the din of subsequent battles has been raised is unnecessary here. It may be sufficient to take haven in the magisterial respecification of the 'Merton thesis' offered by Thomas Kuhn. Kuhn reconceptualizes the 'Puritan/Pietist' label by substituting a broader, and more internalist term, 'Baconian ideology': which refers to an approach in science which stresses empirical research.

analysis of science. Much of the critique of Merton has come from emerging British and European work in the sociology of science which was developed with rather more close-knit ties to the history, philosophy and practice of science (Ben-David, 1978). The Kuhnian approach, which emphasizes the social network framework and cognitive developments around which scientific activity is built, is used as a major base from which to assault the Mertonian paradigm. The Mertonian approach is seen to divert attention away from the way in which social processes impact on the development of scientific products into studying the stratificational and similar aspects of the institutions of science without reference to the actual content of science. The various post-Mertonian, and often anti-Mertonian, conceptions of the sociology of science are more concerned to trace in considerable detail, the complex interplay between cognitive change and social developments.

Mulkay (1979) usefully catalogues several criticisms of his version of Merton's normative model of science (that is, that ". . . the growth of scientific knowledge [is] a consequence of commitment by scientists to such social norms as organised scepticism, disinterestedness, communality and universalism"):—

(1) there is a distinction between what scientists say and what they do;
(2) there is no systematic evidence that scientists do support these norms;
(3) that these norms are not unique to science and to the extent they do operate they are given specific content by particular research groupings;
(4) that the content of scientific activity is external to the inquiry, whereas surely content is central to scientific activities; and

(5) it is difficult to account for intellectual resistance to new ideas from scientists, rather than open-mindedness.

These criticisms cover empirical, theoretical and metatheoretical levels. Each is briefly reviewed.

At an empirical level, some investigations showed that some scientists failed to hold the blandly uniform respectable set of norms Merton was seen as claiming they did. However, Merton's view incorporated a rather more complex model of the set of cultural goals around which the values of science were built: especially given his counterposing of counter-norms to each of the norms of science he had identified. The extent to which the radically different 'interpretative' perspectives of how the normative order of science operates will yield a markedly different picture is yet to come to fruition.

Moreover, evidence of deviance is hardly disconfirming, as the Mertonian analysis of science (1957c) has gone on to show how deviance is actually generated by the operation of the social structures of science.

Kuhn's analysis of science has been used by some critics to attempt to drive a wedge between Merton's emphasis on the role of norms in broadly directing scientific work, and the felt need to also include sociological explanations of the *content* of science. However, Kuhn himself, has resisted being recruited on the side of the anti-Mertonians, saying that this line of criticism is seriously misdirected (1977, p. xxi) and that his own analyses presupposed the existence and role of general scientific values. Nor, can it be shown that Mertonian sociology ignores the content of science: as his own work on the changing foci of scientific attention attests (see the debate initiated by Gieryn, 1982). The 'Kuhnian' influence has clearly been a beneficial impetus to sociology of science, and the question only lies in the extent to which this is compatible with Mertonian sociology.

The third level of reaction lies in the rather different sociological orientations which have been more recently current. From the perspectives of a series of alternative 'interpretative' (micro)sociologies, the Mertonian conception of explaining scientist's behaviour as flowing from their holding of certain abstract values is problematic. Rather, such analyses see these values as cognitive resources to be mobilized in the interpretation of information, the negotiation of shared meanings and the construction of scientific discourse. This emphasis on the linguistic nature of science tends to lead to a strong focus on studying micro-situations. This has led to detailed observation in scientific laboratories, close examination of scientific language and laborious historical reconstruction of the development of specialities. Alongside this has been trenchant critique of received theoreti-

Mertonian sociology of science but able to share the same comfortable revisionist stance towards it. However, until this position is further developed it is difficult to trace its implications.

Merton's programme in the sociology of science is generally perceived as a functional analysis. This is in part because of the central importance placed on values and norms, and the extent to which the actual operation of science is held up against the standard of these ideals. This functional analysis of science explores the ways in which the institutional structure of science has eufunctional or dysfunctional consequences for the cognitive development of science. Critics perceive a strong tendency for the Mertonian analysis of science to then lapse into using the functions of scientific institutions (incorrectly) as explanations of them.

Having briefly surveyed criticisms of Mertonian sociology of science, the question of the relationship of this with his other sociological work is examined. On the whole, Merton develops his sociology of science fairly independently of his general sociology, although he is conscious of a web of linkages between them. Cole and Zuckerman (1975, pp. 160–162) have already drawn attention to several of these continuities between Merton's sociology of science and his general sociology. They suggest that:

"Merton's analysis of competition for priority in science closely parallels his widely known work on deviant behaviour. The origins of deviant behaviour in science and in the larger culture are located in a disjunction between goals and normatively prescribed means. And its incidence depends in large part on the structure of opportunities to conform to the norms. He suggests that the strong emphasis in science on the extension of certified knowledge and thus on original discovery has much the same effect as the comparably strong emphasis in American culture on financial success . . .".

This, then, creates a pressure (itself socially mediated) for possible deviance by scientists in order to achieve this aim.

In addition, they suggest that Merton utilizes in his sociology of science several more aspects of his general approaches:

— analysis of unintended consequences (in this case of the Matthew Effect);
— the maladaptivity of overconforming behaviour;
— self-reinforcing and self-amplifying social processes (e.g. the accumulation of advantage).

This listing of the ways in which Merton's general sociology impinges on his analysis of science is encouraging. Yet, one is struck with the few points which are made, the unconnectedness of the points, and the limited analytical power that is seen to have been imported from Merton's general sociology. In particular, although Cole and Zuckerman follow Merton in involving his anomie theory they apply it only to a discussion of forms of scientific *deviance* which is downplayed as a minor aspect in the actual operation of science. Another central device of alternative modes of adaptation does not seem to be used, although (Lipset and Basu, 1975) develop a somewhat related typology. Stinchcombe (1975), as we have seen, includes comments on Merton's sociology of science in his reworking of Merton's general sociology, so it is clear that he sees a very considerable carry-over of concepts.

Yet, it is possible to show that there is a structural model (along the lines laid out in Chapter 5) embedded within Merton's sociology of science. To be able to construct such a model is crucial to my overall argument given, that Merton worked so long and so recently in this area. Because of this one would expect to find some very strong clues as to his most mature preferences in sociological analysis. Despite the unfavourable auguries from much of the Mertonian programme in this area, Hagstrom (1965) and Storer (1966, 1973) and Ben-David (1971), have begun to build up a structural model of science derived from Merton's work, which has a startlingly complete convergence with his general model, and especially Merton's anomie theory. (This approach has also been briefly reviewed by Knorr–Cetina, 1982, as one of several 'quasi-economic' or 'economic'

equipped to contribute to science. Those in a more disjunctive situation with lesser access to means are subject to more stress and are more likely to be tempted into deviant acts. As well as promoting the production of scientific work, this structure of 'intellectual property' means that steps to claim priority and defend it are also promoted.

Lastly, the results of scientific work have implications which feedback to affect the overall structure of science and related institutions. As Storer has emphasized, this operation of science results in boundary-maintenance in which attempts to subvert the internal recognition–system of science by attempts to obtain recognition from sources outside science are strongly resisted. Stinchcombe adds a slightly finer version of this by pointing up the way in which scientific journals as the premier recognition-granting device are further supported by their continual use.

Dysfunctions for science flow from public disesteem about the negative social consequences of some technological developments. There is even room within Merton's framework for the feedback loops back to social character and interaction environments.

Thus, it is possible to show that Merton's sociology of science nicely matches point-for-point his general structural model (as developed in Chapter 5 above). Indeed, his sociology of science adds two important extra aspects to the general model. His sociology of science raises more clearly the issue of the relationship between institutional and personal goals (cf. Wunderlich, 1979). Science has the institutional goal of the extension of certified knowledge. From this can be derived the personalized version which science holds out to its acolytes of attempting to make *personal* contribution that will extend the frontiers of knowledge. But, the point is, that this institutional analysis must be attempted first, and the personalized version developed from this. The institution will have mechanisms which ensure that people operating within it, are motivated, rewarded and subject to social control that all funnels them towards pursuit of the institutional objectives. The institutional analysis of science draws attention to key features of the institution — especially the conception of 'intellectual property' which relates social rights of ownership to the production of the system.

The importance of including a *prior* institutional analysis, before the remainder of the structural model is set up, is particularly pointed up by the contrasting way in which the theory of anomie was developed. The application of anomie theory to American society centres on the cultural significance of success, especially as operationalized in the fetishized form of financial success. But, where this cultural goal of American society comes from is left hanging in the air. This is partly because Merton has begun his analysis with the *personalized* version of the goal (that is, the form in which it is directed at participants of the society). He does not state the institutional version of this cultural goal. If he had done so, he would have almost certainly been drawn into an explicit Marxian analysis of American Society. If the cultural goal of science is the extension of certified knowledge, then surely the cultural goal of American society is the extension of production. Individuals are constrained to this general purpose by being exhorted to make their own fortune, especially through business ventures. A more explicit accounting for the mode of operation of American society as a capitalist structure would have more firmly secured Merton's analytical schema of deviance, and would have complemented the institutional analysis he sketched for science.

A second contribution to Merton's general sociology from his sociology of science lies in an implicit framework of 'stages of production' of a scientific product that is used. Such a framework has been commonplace in texts on social research methodology, but has been strangely underemployed in the sociology of science itself. As applied in the sociology of science this involves the rather straightforward idea that the extent and type of the influence of either external or internal sources depends on the stage involved. Merton's conception is not explicitly developed, but at least distinguishes between:

— the problem-selection phase (at the collective level the areas of attention of a field: see Zuckerman, 1977);
— the internal organization of the production of a scientific work (especially the theory-choices and methods — choices made in the process of working through a study);

seen as a straightforward product of its ethos. As far as I can see, it seems that *both* critics, his own disciples and even Merton himself inadequately grasped the radical implications of his own 1957 reformulation of his model. The disciples were concerned with developing a quantitative description of the social organization of science which diverted them from key theoretical issues, while their methodology resonated more readily with a combination of the earlier model and the work of Price and Kuhn. The critics became locked into the earlier model because it fitted with their own interests in the cognitive and ideational aspects of scientist's work. And for Merton himself, it was partly a case of 'je ne suis pas Mertoniste' and partly his eclectic ability to become absorbed into the problematics of others.

6.3 OTHER SUBSTANTIVE CONTRIBUTIONS

Merton's substantive contributions were hardly confined to the two areas reviewed so far. In several other of the areas he has worked he has contributed material not only of particular interest to those working in that field, but also of relevance to his general sociology. Unfortunately, there is room here for only the briefest of reviews.

In his early contributions to the sociology of organizations, which nicely brought sociological attention to bear on this central feature of modern societies by refurbishing Weber's classic model, Merton sets up his own model of the internal functioning of organizations which nicely fits his overall schema. This is particularly brought out in March and Simon's (1958) formalization of this work. This beginning of formal modelling of the relationship among the different components of an organization was carried further, through the collection of an important reader on bureaucracy (Merton, 1952a) and by monographs from Merton's students Selznick, Gouldner, Lipset and Trow and Blau (for discussions see Mouzelis, 1967; Pinder and Moore, 1980).

Alongside his work on organizations, Merton developed material in the sociology of occupations and then was involved in a large-scale study which, from the client institutions' viewpoint was evaluating the effects of changing curricula in several prestigious medical schools, and from the sociologists' viewpoint was involved in tracing the adult and professional socialization process of medical students as structured by the cultural and social structures of the medical schools (Merton, 1957a). In this study, much of Merton's status-and-role theory conceptualization was used to guide the analysis of the data, but it was not really used as an experimental test-bed for these ideas. Later work on the sociology of occupations and the sociology of altruism arose out of a ten-year long consultation with the American Nurses' Association (several essays from this are included in Merton, 1982).

Another important area of study lay in urban sociology, with Merton's analyses of community influentials, local–cosmopolitan orientations and friendship networks.

Merton's work has been laced through with substantial attention to methodology and also to the sociology of knowledge. In the methodology area Merton has continually been sensitive to the relevance of data-sources and data-analysis procedures which will better test theory, and has gone out of his way to draw attention to developments, as well as himself assist in the development of some (especially "the focused interview"). The sociology of knowledge has been a similar long-standing interest in which Merton has been able to provide useful reviews of relevant material, but has not been able to develop (undoubtedly much to his own disappointment), a sustained empirically-based theoretical programme that would lure this field away from its philosophical predilections and into cumulative building of knowledge about the relationships between cultural structures and their social bases. This lack in the development of a Mertonian sociology of knowledge leaves a lacuna in the overall schema sketched in Chapter 5, as it means that several crucial links remain sufficiently explored.

6.4   CONCLUSION

To a considerable extent Merton's range of interests have been rounded and interpenetrating, although he seldom made a virtue of this. His sociology of knowledge bracketed his sociology of science and sociology of social science and alongside these lay his interests in methodology. While

embedded in the substantive approaches were overlooked. Thus the cumulative impact was not realized, and the general model in turn lacked fine-tuning from the results of the more substantive analyses.

7

Merton and the ghost of Marx

In his *A Sociology of Sociology,* Friedrichs (1970) argues that the most important paradigms which undergird sociology are its moral stances, and he goes on to identify 'prophetic' versus 'priestly' modes of conducting sociology. A somewhat similar distinction, but one expressed at the conceptual rather than moral level, is made in other writings (e.g. Mills, 1959; Gouldner, 1970), and this point is clearly posed in the epigraph (from Gouldner) used to open this book. The force of these moral and conceptual concerns is overlapping and reinforcing.

As well as influencing the methodological and the theoretical stances of mid-century sociology, Merton also influenced its moral tone, and its stance towards the deficiencies of the existing social order. This can be particularly seen in the way Merton handles issues of social class, exploitation, repression and similar concerns that have, rightly in my opinion, been central to any sociological perspective of any depth. The way Merton relates to the Marxian heritage of sociology may be a crucial test of his view of the moral stance sociology should take, and the extent to which it should employ critical explanations of exploitation, suffering and the structural locations of power.

In his critical review commentary on the Festschrift for Merton edited by Coser, Randall Collins argues that: "If there is a central theme that underlies virtually all of Merton's work, I would say it is the effort to de-fuse stratificational issues. . . . structural inequalities are simply settings for the drama of social mobility" (Collins, 1977, p. 153).

Collins argues that Merton holds a 'liberal' ideological stance and that the logic of his approach is to transform issues involving social conflict or political domination into abstract analyses that nicely show how such aspects really are part of a self-equilibrating status quo. This, he feels, has operated out from a definite ideological stance, a weaker version of this critique suggests that Merton's work operated with a more diffuse ideological tone, that in particular had made too comfortable an alliance with 'established interests'. Gouldner (1961) in his famous essay entitled "anti-Minotaur, the myth of a value-free sociology" draws attention to differences he sees between 'professional' compared to 'intellectual' approaches to sociology by comparing the 'Columbia/Harvard' [and notably therefore Merton] and 'Chicago' styles of studying medical institutions.

> It is difficult to escape the feeling that the former are more respectful of the medical establishment than the Chicagoans, that they more readily regard it in terms of its own claims, and are more prone to view it as a noble profession. Chicagoans, however, tend to be uneasy about the idea of a 'profession' as a tool for study, believing instead that the notion of an 'occupation' provides more basic guidelines for study, and arguing that occupations as diverse as the nun and the prostitute, or the plumber and the physician, reveal instructive sociological similarities. Chicagoans seem more likely to take a secular view of medicine, seeing it as an occupation much like any other and are somewhat more inclined towards debunking forays into the seamier side of medical practise. Epitomizing this difference are the very differences in the book titles that the two groups have chosen for their medical studies. Harvard and Columbia have soberly called two of their most important works, 'The Student-Physician' and 'Experiment Perilous', while the Chicagoans have irreverently labelled their own recent study of medical students, the 'Boys in White'. (Gouldner, 1961, pp. 76, 77)

Another line of criticism has involved a rather more lofty annoyance that Merton's sharpening of analytical tools has vulgarized conceptualizations handed down from classic writers. Thus, for example, Bryan Turner argues (without any serious reflection on Merton's work) that:

the bland Mertonian conception of 'unanticipated consequences' and 'latent functions' . . . does not capture the evil ambience of Weber's theory of routinisation. It is not simply that purposive actions have consequences which are not recognised by social actors; the outcome of human actions often work against social actors in such a way as to limit or reduce the scope of their freedom (Turner, 1981, pp. 9, 10).

Similarly, Horton (1964) had earlier made a rather more engaged criticism that Merton's attention to anomie had confused the very different concepts of alienation and anomie and involved a "transformation from radical to conformist definitions and values under the guise of value-free sociology".

Some aspects of Merton's image of sociology might have had the effect of curbing the interest of sociologists in active involvement in social issues: for example, Merton is sharp to defend professional sociology from confusion with political journalism, and he makes a point of demarcating C. Wright Mills's later polemical writings from his earlier scholarly work (Merton, 1968b, p. 66). Another instance is that in his two main interventions in international forums of sociology ("Social Conflict in Styles of Sociological Work" and "Insiders and Outsiders") the effect of Merton's addresses is to attempt to smooth over and smother differences, to see lines of conflict as useful divisions-of-labour within the whole sociological enterprise. Indeed, in terms of his own sociology of knowledge (see above: Chapter 4), in which he suggests that views which emphasize the complexities and complications of social life tend to be held by conservative groups, Merton himself (along with almost the whole of the sociological enterprise) seems to stand self-accused.

Lastly, it can be pointed out that Merton's sociology is vulnerable to criticism as having 'conservative' undertones, because his conceptual armament lacks theoretical resources in those areas of sociology most needed to address such issues. Even such a sympathetic critic as Stinchcombe points out that "aside from information determinants of this placement in the flow of rewards and punishments . . . Merton has not systematically analyzed power systems and their implications" (Stinchcombe, 1975, p. 23). However, he does note that the development of "a

locus for gathering the resources for overthrowing the class structure. In Merton's study of community influentials, class is seen as a base, around which different forms of local influence are wielded. In later studies, the structure of stratification in science is at the centre of many analyses. Perhaps, most dramatically, the careful comparison of similarities between Marxian and functional analyses in Merton's 1949 essay on functional analysis is replaced in his 1975 essay on 'structural analysis' with an explicit if unspecified commitment to the Marxian theoretical approach as a central component in structural analysis. Further Marxian concern can be found behind Merton's sketch of a sociology of knowledge, and even in his setting up of status-and-role analysis.

Merton's exposure to, and use of, Marxian thought remains somewhat mysterious. Coser refers to Merton's "continued focus on class factors which had been stimulated by his immersion in Marxian thought" (Coser, 1975, p. 95), to his "profound knowledge of the Marxian canon" (Coser and Nisbet, 1975, p. 7), and to the considerable influence of the New Deal 'revolution' that captured the political imagination of that generation (just as Gouldner had emphasized these points). So, it is clear that Merton was exposed to Marxian thought. In this study it has been possible to point to several places where a distinctly Marxian frame has been employed. Moreover, Merton had the courage to continue to use Marxian terms, even during a period when Barber (1952) felt that the term 'communism' used to describe one of the key norms of science, might be more tactfully replaced by 'communality'.

How did Merton actually use the Marxian canon? Coser is quick to point out that Merton carefully attempted to turn any Marxian ideological thrusts to analytical purpose, stripped of any value-laden freight.

Moreover, Gouldner suggests that Merton "sought to make peace between Marxism and Functionalism precisely by emphasizing their affinities, and thus make it easier for marxist students to become Functionalists" (Gouldner, 1970, p. 335). (Merton protests in reply that "I had neither the far-seeing intent nor the wit and powers thus to transmogrify my students": 1976b, p. 123).

Such a 'class reading' of Merton's work has a limited basis. Much of Merton's work is alert to stratificational issues, but then slips by them. For example, in his study of medical school a conceptual note on 'socialization' contrasts sociological usage with "the doctrine which advocates the owner-ship and control of the apparatus of production by the community as a whole, and its administration by political agencies of the community" (1957a, p. 289). There is no comment on how this principle might work in the medical context, or any alerting the reader to the way in which medical services are organized in capitalist societies around the opposing principle. Despite writing a methodological critique of class scales (1943a) and occasionally drawing on class explanations, Merton nearly always slides into treating them as strata, and indicates that he identifies them with Weberian rather than Marxian marker characteristics (e.g. 1968b, pp. 469–474). Although Merton is critical of some aspects of the Davis–Moore functional analysis of social stratification (its assumption about the univer-sality of religious institutions: Merton, 1968b, pp. 96–100) he does not confront the central assumptions of this theory, and it is specifically and very carefully incorporated in Mertonian sociology of science (e.g. Cole and Cole, 1973; Cole, 1979; Zuckerman, 1976). To be blunt, Merton's conceptual frameworks afford little purchase on the Marxian concerns identified above, and nor do they easily connect up with types of analysis which might give them such critical bite.

To some extent this sliding past any conceptual confrontation of class and related issues is set within a broader reluctance to engage in macro-sociological issues. As Nelson (1972) points out in belatedly reviewing *Science, Technology and Society in Seventeenth Century England* Merton failed to continue his early interest in the 'historical sociology of culture'. However, Nelson seems to feel that there are signs that Merton might be about to re-engage at this scale of analysis. Indeed, he has: but rather in the form of his historical studies of the development of images such as *On the Shoulders of Giants*.

7.2 MERTON'S VALUES STANCE

Merton is far too sensitive to the complex relationship between values and the scientific enterprise to take a simplistic stance on the social responsibili-

relative. It is not tied to any absolute standard, which would be Utopian, but to a standard of what, so far as we know, could be accomplished under attainable conditions. When we say that a group or community or society is disorganized, we mean that its structure of statuses and roles is "not working as effectively as it might to achieve valued purposes". Taylor *et al,* (1973, pp. 95, 96) develop their view that:

> Merton's ideal or perfect society would be one in which there was an accord between merit and its consequences. The means for achieving success would be respected, and the opportunities open to all those of sufficient merit. The motivation to compete and the opportunities to succeed would be in proportion to the degree of individual stratification necessary for the society to function. The competition for success, furthermore, would be enjoyed as an end in itself, and the cultural goals would be substantial and definite — rather than fetishistic and relativistic.

Although this model is developed out of Merton's writings on anomie, it is certainly also applicable to his implicit moral analysis of the institution of science.

Merton develops the outline of a moral stance for sociology, especially in the last chapter of *Mass Persuasion*. His alertness to the close links between technical problems and moral dilemmas is brought out in his argument that:

> the initial formulation of [any] scientific investigation [is] conditioned

by the implied values of the scientist. Thus,had the investigator been orientated toward such democratic values as respect for the dignity of the individual, he would have framed his scientific problem differently. . . . He would be, in short, sensitized to certain questions stemming from his democratic values which would otherwise be readily overlooked (1946, p. 188).

In a later discussion Merton sees sociology as "link[ed] up with a critical morality as opposed to conventional reality" (1976a, p. 38). Clearly, an 'activist' value stance towards the recognition of social problems is preferred to a fatalist stance of passive acceptance of 'sadistic social structures' ("which are so organized as to systematically inflict pain, humiliation, suffering and deep frustration on particular groups and strata", 1976a, p. 131) — if only because fatalism is frequently generated by such social structures and works in the class interests of the privileged against the depressed. This framework builds around the best ways of "serv[ing] the ultimate values of society" (1976a, p. 40). However, this notion is itself problematic, and is not adequately developed.

So, as with his avoidance of close attention to social class issues, Merton also falters in developing an explicit moral stance. His denigration of simple moral views is not coupled with a drive to erect, or even encourage the erection of, a more sophisticated moral framework. Unintentionally perhaps, and as an undeliberate consequence of his discipline-building concerns, Merton has perhaps fallen into a position he himself had criticized, similar to that of the engineer who has "come to be indoctrinated with an ethical sense of limited responsibilities" in which responsibility is disclaimed for "attending to the ways in which . . . knowledge was applied" (1947a [1968b, p. 622]).

7.3   CONCLUSION

Despite these two 'flaws' in his sociological enterprise, as seen from this particular critical perspective, Merton has bequeathed an analytical apparatus for the study of sociological problems and alongside this has helped to shape the disciplinary matrix of American sociology which has to some considerable extent developed this cumulative sociological knowledge. Perhaps it is for others to develop these and thus to attend more closely to macrosociological concerns and social criticism. Moreover, it might be argued that his sociology retained enough of a radical impulse to keep this perspective alive within sociology during the darkness of the McCarthy era.

In this concluding chapter, I return to attempt answers to the questions posed at the beginning of this book: of how the clearly significant impact of Merton on sociology is to be interpreted and what its long-term impact is likely to be.

In the literature, there are four main lines of interpretation of the nature and extent of Merton's influence. They all agree in recognizing that Merton has exerted a considerable influence on sociology, but differ in their interpretation of this influence.

8.1.1 Merton as orthodox

The 'orthodox' interpretation places Merton as a junior partner of Parsons in the 'structural-functionalist' enterprise. At best, a difference between the two is recognized in terms of the tactics of constructing sociology: 'grand' theory versus 'middle order' theory. If pressed, those adopting this viewpoint might point to any, or several, of a wide array of concepts particularly associated with Merton: reference-groups, role-sets, etc.

However, in this orthodox view, no underlying relationship between these concepts is recognized. In effect, this viewpoint leaves the possibility of any general viewpoint underlying Merton's contributions relatively unexamined and unexplained.

8.1.2 Merton as ultra-orthodox

A second line of interpretation sees Merton as rather more separate from the general 'structural-functionalist' mould: but no less 'dangerous' for this. This line of interpretation is grounded in radical sociological theory and has been advanced particularly by Randall Collins. It is interesting that Collins has openly argued against Merton, whereas several predecessors in this tradition chose not to: C. Wright Mills excluding Merton from attack amidst his general critique of sociology (see Horowitz, 1983), Alvin Gouldner being rent by ambivalence and Irving Horowitz (who attempted to take up Mills's mantle) being cited in Garfield (1977) as full of praise for Merton. Collins largely agrees with the first line of interpretation in according Merton a leadership role in the 1940s and 1950s, although he apportions away some of Merton's apparent impact. Collins argues specifically that "it seems apparent that his eminence in [sociology of science] is not due to his having organized a workable paradigm" but also intends this statement to hold more generally. Instead, Collins feels that the resonances of Merton's work sat well with the liberal pathos of the Cold War period but that it is limited in its long-term significance because it was not grounded in what Collins regards as key explanatory factors and (ironically, given Merton's own methodological writings) because it consequently diverts attention from explanatory strategies towards typological exercises. In this book I have taken up some of the challenges from this viewpoint, underlining several while also indicating that the Mertonian approach has considerably more merit than Collins supposes. Paradoxically, Collins's own sociology of Merton's sociology is rather too clever: Merton is successful either scientifically (because his work appeals to fellow sociologists) or socially (because it has an appeal for some policy-makers). How else? What might seem to most to be virtue is simply read as vice.

8.1.3   Merton as a 'cautious rebel'

Taylor *et al.* (1973) characterize Merton as a cautious rebel because they feel that he is prepared to make definite, if limited, social judgements. A similar position with respect to his theory has been advanced by the group of writers in the late 1960s and early 1970s that saw Merton as centred in a structural perspective adjacent to Parsonian functional analysis, although they had difficulty in explicating what was involved in this position. (Interestingly, Merton would probably locate himself in this group.)

8.1.4   Merton as an unintended general theorist

A fourth line of interpretation is that most seriously advanced by Stinchcombe in which he argues that Merton's influence has been won by his implicit 'general theory'. This interpretation develops from the earlier weaker version. In this book I have attempted to develop a stronger version of this approach by attempting to show that Merton's general model incorporated rather more of Merton's work than Stinchcombe had sup-

— power/fruitfulness: Stinchcombe addresses two particular arguments in support of the ability of Merton's general theory to be useful in tackling a variety of empirical problems, its power in the destructive criticism of alternative viewpoints (e.g. those of Malinowski or Sorokin), and its attention to both the stability and disruption in social patterns and to processes of social magnification or amplification.

— economy: Merton obtains economy at a trivial level by writing on one topic at a time, and more importantly by generating a variety of specific theories from a small set of common elements.

— precision: Merton's theories are made more easily testable because, although couched in terms of clear and general conceptual 'scales', which cover the full range of the full dimension, Merton also points to different surface forms in which theoretically relevant differences appear. The theoretical language is consonant with the grammar of empirical research testing.

Stinchcombe's criticism of Merton's theory is a brilliant, if at times somewhat bewildering, *tour de force*. In order to build a more systematic critical stance, we need a more systematic framework through which we can look at a theory at the levels of: its underlying imagery, its formal qualities and its presentation — in terms of social philosophy, philosophy of science and literary criticism. Stinchcombe has shown that at the levels of theory-building and the aesthetics of theory-presentation Merton's work has widespread appeal. But his point about the attractiveness of the underlying imagery needs more development.

In the endemic sociological struggle to incorporate both agency and structure (both free will and determinism) in theoretical formulations Merton favours emphasizing the importance of structure and yet accords people a significant role. Merton's actors are depicted as striving, motivated and reacting to the social forces structuring their activities. As his use of the concept of 'sociological ambivalence' attests, Merton's sociology allows individuals a range (albeit socially circumscribed) of choice. This is pointed up in his writing by the frequent use of personal testimony, usually gleaned from biographical material, that are central illustrative material in his accounts. Merton's conception of 'man' is rather more socialized than that of Durkheim or Freud, who posit social structure as mere curbs on biological and psychological impulses, and Merton rather sees people as socially motivated and channelled as well as curbed. Nevertheless, while Merton has room for the agency of individuals, his focus remains unrelentingly on social structures and their operation. Stinchcombe puts this in an interesting way in arguing that "Merton's theoretical structure provides multiple opportunities to move back and forth from striving or thalamic men to social structural outcomes" and that this is made possible "by modifying the structural concepts so that people fit as natural parts of them" (Stinchcombe, 1975, p. 27). In building a workable accommodation of the central concern about 'structure' and 'agency' (cf. Giddens, 1984) into his theory Merton has been able to provide a balanced working platform from which to build good sociology.

Similarly, Merton's approach has been able to provide a workable accommodation with some of the other antinomies which afflict the enterprise of social theory (for example the macro-/micro- distinction, the link between sociology and psychology or the sometimes-feigned dichotomy between history and sociology). Although his attempts to tackle the central theoretical problems of sociology are seldom explicit, in fact I feel, he has attempted to come to grips with most of the central issues, and it is this quality of his work which ensures its continued significance for sociology. However, this claim needs extended and careful theoretical critique, which is not attempted here.

It is clear that Merton largely works within a 'social order' metaphor of society (in which the prime but not the only task of the theory is to 'explain' the obvious empirical generalization that there is very considerable continuance of the social order). It is also clear that the mood of his work is largely optimistic (in that the flaws in social structures are not overwhelming). But despite these general commitments to order and optimism, it is also clear that Merton's sociology is rather more complex than this. In particular, Merton's writing has been able to avoid the full limitations of the

were made so that a popular image of sociology became its face as social survey research. Alongside the fine-tuning of survey research as a research tool came its conversion from a merely descriptive device into a research tool for testing sociological explanations, and at least some attempts to incorporate both more sensitivity to patterns of social meanings (such as through focused interviewing) and more structural considerations onto its aggregate social psychology. And the whole was enveloped within a developing codification of methodological principles. This is well known, although the usual accounts do not sufficiently stress the ways in which sociological theory was built into the empirical methods. Merton not only usefully contributed to some of these methodological developments, but he also had a role — through working closely with important methodologists, especially Lazarsfeld — in ensuring that data-collection and data-analysis models were consonant with social theory. Rather more importantly, he played a major part in recruiting ideas from the classical traditions of sociological thought, stripping them of their wider philosophical coating and putting them to work in building sociological explanations.

Alongside the building-up of the empirical foundation of sociology there was the laying down (under the label of functional and structural analysis) of a broad theoretical approach which focused attention on social structures, albeit those at an intermediate rather than a societal level: social phenomena such as occupational groups, organizations and communities. Use of a 'functional' form of (pseudo-) explanation was actually an infrequent mark of this broad approach, although it was a heuristic methodological device which ensured that a structural level of analysis was attended to, alongside an interest in social psychology. In short, American social theory in the post-World War II period was rather more complex than labels such as functionalist or empiricist suggest, and it was subject to a wider range of central influence than that imparted by Parsons alone. While Merton was only one of several theoretical writers prominent in this period, examination of his work inevitably 'thickens' and deepens our appreciation of the complexities of this key period in the development of sociology.

Since the heyday of 'structural-functionalism' there has been more sustained attention to both more sophisticated interpretative and radical sociologies while those continuing the mainstream have split up into an array of more particular theories which are closely linked to particular methodologies — network analysis, causal modelling etc. (see Mullins, 1973). These more specific neo-positivist approaches are more closely driven by their methodological underpinnings and have lost many of the wider theoretical concerns that informed the broad sociological tradition in which they were nurtured. The theoretical material developed under the 'structure-functional' mode of sociological analysis in the early period of post-World War II sociology still provides the conceptual infrastructure for more recent sociology, although it is not always easy to uncover this.

The interpretative and radical sociologies — each also split into a range of alternative approaches — have by now developed to some depth. Yet, as they do so, it is interesting to note that they are increasingly riven by revisionist breakaway groups who seek some form of *rapprochement* with mainstream sociology.

Some interpretative sociologies seek to build up from what is often an ethnographic or microsociological foundation to explore dominances built into widely embracing cultural structures, or to pull back from a purely 'ideational' level of analysis to also examine the social structures which 'carry' the cultural forms. Some Marxian sociologists are concerned to build a more social adjunct to the analysis of the economic machinery of capitalism which so dominated the later writings of Marx. At the level of empirical research there are also signs of some convergence amongst the mosaic of theoretical programmes presently constituting sociology. Not only are there more signs of commitment to the need for social reseach, but also some interest in working through to mutually understood positions on the appropriateness of particular research tools. If I am correct in distinguishing signs of a pulling together of a variety of strands of sociology (albeit at a considerably higher level of theoretical sophistication and a deeper awareness of the perils of eclecticism) sociologists could do well to reflect upon the earlier accommodation made in Merton's sociology to a variety of approaches which often appear so remotely separated. Not only is it important that Merton's sociology be closely examined in order to see how the accommodation was effected, and whether the joins held, but also identifying a good sociological problem — one that has significant implications for theory — and to learn what constitutes an appropriate theoretical solution to a problem" (Merton, 1968b, p. 36).

Epilogue: a battery of ironies in relation to Merton

Stinchcombe has remarked that the sense of irony in Merton's writing is one of its compelling features.

> Merton clearly likes irony. He is most pleased to find motives of advancing knowledge creating priority conflicts amongst scientists, and hardly interested in the fact that such motives also advance knowledge. He likes to find political bosses helping people while good government types turn a cold shoulder. He likes to find Sorokin offering statistics on ideas to combat the empiricist bent of modern culture and to urge an idealist logico-meaningful analysis of ideas. He likes to range Engels and functionalists down parallel columns to show them really to be the same (Stinchcombe, 1975, p. 28).

Schneider (1975) has also called attention to this aspect of Mertonian sociology. Merton's intellectual career has also been attended by irony.

A strong theme in writing this study has been its 'self-exemplifying' aspect (cf., for example, Merton's, 1977, comments on the 'self-exemplifying features of the sociology of science'). These pages teem with Merton's concepts and terminology, not only in the reporting of the substance of his work but also in the analysing of it. This includes general categories, but also categories fine-tuned to handle academic contexts. Indeed, Merton himself has devoted much effort to analysing the social mechanisms involved with the generation and transmission of knowledge (e.g. his

linked in with ongoing work, Parsons's work retained an obstinant unique-ness that at least partly resisted incorporation in ongoing systematic social theory, but left important traces for historical study.

Since Merton's methodological doctrines stressed 'middle-range' theory it was hardly expected that he would produce theory of general sociological significance. Yet, as this study has argued, this has been the effect of his work. But, strangely, this general theoretical impact has not been in the form of 'functional analysis' but, rather, in the form of a structural analysis. As argued above (Chapter 4) Merton, ironically, may have undermined the very mode of analysis he was attempting to advance.

Although Merton prided himself on the clarity and strength of his argumentation, this very clarity of his formal work seems to have provoked further elaboration or reworking of his models. For example, several writers (e.g. Dubin, 1959) have been concerned to rework one or other of Merton's logical typologies to generate a more complex internal logical structure. Many of these attempts exploit weaknesses or inadequacies in Merton's original formulations, although some are clearly straightforward extensions. Others (e.g. Mulkay, 1971) have complained about the lack of precision in Merton's work. There has been even some detailed criticism by Matza of the cavalier rhetoric through which Merton, in his essay on anomie, eliminated the pathological image of deviance central to earlier views by dismissing it without attention (Matza, 1969, pp. 58, 59) and the cleverness with which data on the reliability of official crime statistics was handled by citing the relevant study and then ignoring it (1969, p. 97). Few analysts whose signature has been the explicitness of their argument have had such detailed attention paid to the deficiencies of their rhetoric!

Perhaps the deepest irony is that Merton, himself a scientist of the highest repute (Sztompka has suggested he should be nominated for a Nobel Prize, were there one in sociology), has engaged, with Harriet Zuckerman, in a study of the social situation of highly prestigious scientists. It is fitting to reflect on the extent to which his summary of the working style of Nobel prizewinners fits Merton's own operating approach. (This passage forms an appropriate epilogue.)

Even when some of his contributions have been independently made by an aggregate of other scientists, the great scientist serves distinctive functions. It required a Freud, for instance, to focus the attention of many psychologists upon a wide array of ideas, which, as has been shown elsewhere, had in large part also been hit upon by various other scientists. Such focalizing may turn out to be a distinctive function of eminent men and women of science.

It is not so much that these great men of science pass on their techniques, methods, information and theory to novices working with them. More consequentially, they convey to their associates the norms and values that govern significant research. Often in their later years, or after their death, this personal influence becomes routinized, in the fashion described by Max Weber for other fields of human activity. Charisma becomes institutionalized, in the forms of schools of thought and research establishments.

Though attentive to the cues provided by the work of others in their field, the Nobelists are self-directed investigators, moving confidently into new fields of inquiry once they are persuaded that a previous one has been substantially mined. In these activities they display a high degree of venturesome fortitude. They are prepared to tackle important though difficult problems rather than settle for easy and secure ones.

Confident in their powers of discriminating judgment — a confidence that has been confirmed by the responses of others to their previous work — they tend, in their exposition, to emphasize and develop the central ideas and findings and to play down peripheral ones. This serves to highlight the significance of their contributions.

Finally, this character structure and an acquired set of high standards often lead these outstanding scientists to discriminate between work that is worth publishing and that which, in their candid judgment, is best left unpublished though it could easily find its way into print.

This in turn reinforces the expectation of their fellow scientists that what these eminent scientists publish (at least during their most productive period) will be worth close attention. The more closely other

Bibliography

MERTON'S PUBLICATIONS REFERRED TO

1934a   Recent French Sociology. *Social Forces*, **12**, 537–545.

1934b   Durkheim's Division of Labour in Society. *American Journal of Sociology*, **40**, 319–328.

1936a   Civilization and Culture. *Sociology and Social Research*, **21**, 103–113.

1936b   The Unanticipated Consequences of Purposive Social Action. *American Sociological Review*, **1**, 894–904. 1976b, 145–155.

1937   Social Time: A Methodological and Functional Analysis (with Pitirim A. Sorokin). *American Journal of Sociology*, **42**, 615–629.

1938a   Science, Technology and Society in Seventeenth Century England. In *Osiris: Studies on the History and Philosophy of Science, and on the History of Learning and Culture*. George Sarton (ed.). The St. Catherine Press, Bruges, Belgium, pp. 362–632 (with new Preface, Howard Ferig, New York, 1970; Harper & Row, New York, 1970).

1938b   Social Structure and Anomie. *American Sociological Review*, **3**, 672–682. 1968b, 185–214.

1938c   Science and the Social Order. *Philosophy of Science*, **5**, 321–337. 1968b, 591–603; 1973, 254–266.

1939a   Bureaucratic Structure and Personality. *Social Forces*, **18**, 560–68. 1968b, 249–260.

1939b   Fact and Factiousness in Ethnic Opinionnaires. *American Sociological Review*, **5**(1), 13–28. 1976b, 251–269.

1941a   Florian Znaniecki's 'The Social Role of the Man of Knowledge': a review essay. *American Sociological Review*, **6**, 111–115. 1973, 41–46.

1941b   Intermarriage and the Social Structure: Fact and Theory. *Psychiatry*, **4**, 361–374. 1973, 217–250.

1942   A Note on Science and Democracy. *Journal of Legal and Political Sociology*, **1**, 115–126. Science and the Democratic Social Structure. 1968b, 604–615; The Normative Structure of Science. 1973, 267–278; 1982a, 3–16.

1943a   The Formation of Scales of Socioeconomic Status: A Comment (with Genevieve Knupfer). *Rural Sociology* **8**, 236–239.

1943b   Studies in Radio and Film Propaganda (with Paul Lazarsfeld).

1947a The Machine, the Worker, and the Engineer. *Science*, **105**, 79–81. 1968b, 616–627.

1947b Selected Problems of Field Work in the Planned Community. *American Sociological Review*, **12**, 304–312.

1948a The Position of Sociological Theory. *American Sociological Review*, **13**, 164–168.

1948b The Bearing of Empirical Research on the Development of Sociological Theory. *American Sociological Review*, **13**, 505–515. 1968b, 156–171.

1948c Discrimination and the American Creed. In R. M. MacIver (ed.), *Discrimination and National Welfare*. Harper and Brothers, New York, pp. 66–126. 1973, 189–216.

1948d The Self-Fulfilling Prophecy. *Antioch Review*, (Summer), 193–210. 1968b, 475–490; 1982a, 248–268.

1949a Patterns of Influence: A Study of Interpersonal Influence and Communication Behaviour in a Local Community. In Paul F. Lazarsfeld and Frank Stanton (eds.), *Communications in Research, 1948-49*. Harper and Brothers, New York, 180–219. 1968b, 441–474.

1949b Manifest and Latent Functions. In *Social Theory and Social Structure*. 1968b, 73–138.

1949c The Role of Applied Social Science in the Formation of Policy. *Philosophy of Science* **16**, 161–181. Technical and Moral Dimensions of Policy Research. 1973, 70–98.

1950 Contributions to the Theory of Reference Group Behaviour (with Alice S. Rossi). In Continuities in Social Research: Studies in the *Scope and Method of 'The American Soldier'* (edited with Paul F. Lazarsfeld). The Free Press, New York. 1968b, 279–334.

1952a   *Reader in Bureaucracy* (edited with Ailsa P. Gray, Barbara Hockey and Hanan C. Selvin). The Free Press, New York.

1952b   Foreword to Bernard Barber, *Science and the Social Order*. The Free Press, New York, pp. xi–xxiii. The Neglect of the Sociology of Science. 1973, 210–220.

1953   Foreword to Hans Gerth and C. Wright Mills, *Character and Social Structure*. Harcourt Brace Jovanovich, New York, pp. vii–ix.

1954   Friendship as a Social Process: A Substantive and Methodological Analysis (with Paul Lazarsfeld). In Morroe Berger, Theodore Abel and Charles Page (eds.), *Freedom and Control in Modern Society*. Van Nostrand, New York, pp. 18–66.

1955   The Socio-Cultural Environment and Anomie. In H. L. Witmer and R. Kotinsky (eds.), *Perspectives for Research on Juvenile Delinquency*. U.S. Government Printing Office, Washington D.C., pp. 24–50.

1956   *The Focused Interview* (with Marjorie Fiske and Patricia L. Kendall). The Free Press, New York.

1957a   Some Preliminaries to a Sociology of Medical Education. In Robert K. Merton, George G. Reader and Patricia L. Kendall (eds.), *The Student Physician*. Harvard University Press, Cambridge, Mass., pp. 3–79. 1982a, 135–198.

1957b   The Role-Set: Problems in Sociological Theory. *British Journal of Sociology*, **8**, 2, 106–20.

1957c   Priorities in Scientific Discovery: a chapter in the sociology of science. *American Sociological Review*, **22**(6), 635–659. 1973, 286–324.

1957d   *The Freedom to Read: Perspective and Program* (with Richard McKeon and Walter Gellhorn). R. R. Bowker Co., New York.

1958   Functions of the Professional Association. *American Journal of Nursing*, **58**, 50–54. 1982a, 199–209.

1959a   Notes on Problem-Finding in Sociology. In Robert K. Merton, Leonard Broom and Leonard S. Cottrell, Jr. (eds.), *Sociology Today*. Basic Books, New York, pp. ix–xxxiv. 1982a, 17–42.

1959b   Social Conformity, Deviation and Opportunity Structures. *American Sociological Review*, **24**, 2, 177–89.

1959c   The Scholar and the Craftsman. In Marshall Clagett (ed.), *Critical Problems in the History of Science*. University of Wisconsin Press, Madison, pp. 24–29.

1960   The Ambivalences of Le Bon's The Crowd (introduction to the Compass Edition of Gustave Le Bon, *The Crowd*). Viking Press, New York, pp. v–xxxix.

1961a   Social Conflict in Styles of Sociological Work. *Transactions, Fourth World Congress of Sociology*, **3**, 21–46. 1973, 47–69.

       Theory and Social Structure. 1968b, 1–38.

1967b On Sociological Theories of the Middle Range. In *Social Theory and Social Structure*. 1968b, 39–72.

1967c *On Theoretical Sociology: Five Essays, Old and New*. The Free Press, New York. (Incorporated in the 1968 edition of *Social Theory and Social Structure*.)

1968a The Matthew Effect in Science: the Reward and Communication Systems of Science are Considered. *Science*, **199**, 55–63. 1973, 325–342.

1968b *Social Theory and Social Structure*. Free Press, Glencoe (earlier editions 1949 and 1957).

1969 Foreword to a Preface for an Introduction to a Prologomenon to a Discourse on a Certain Subject. *American Sociologist*, **4**, 99.

1970 Preface: to 1970 edition of *Science, Technology and Society in Seventeenth Century England*, pp. vii–xxix. Social and Cultural Contexts of Science. 1973, 173–190.

1971 The Precarious Foundations of Detachment in Sociology. In Edward A. Tiryakian (ed.), *The Phenomenon of Sociology*. Appleton-Century-Crofts, New York, pp. 188–199.

1972a Insiders and Outsiders: A Chapter in the Sociology of Knowledge. (Revised edn.). *American Journal of Sociology* (July), 9–47. The Perspectives of Insiders and Outsiders. 1973, 99–136.

1972b On Discipline Building: The Paradoxes of George Sarton (with Arnold Thackray). *ISIS*, **63**, 219, 473–495.

1973 *The Sociology of Science: Theoretical and Empirical Investigations*. (edited by Norman Storer). University of Chicago Press, Chicago.

1975a Structural Analysis in Sociology. In Peter M. Blau (ed.),

Approaches to the Study of Social Structure. The Free Press, New York, pp. 21–52. 1976b, 109–144.

1975b   Thematic Analysis in Science: Notes on Holton's Concept. *Science*, **188** (April 25), 335–338.

1976a   Social Problems and Sociological Theory. In Robert K. Merton and Robert A. Nisbet (eds.), *Contemporary Social Problems.* Harcourt Brace Jovanovich, New York (previous editions: 1961, 1966, 1971), pp. 3–43.

1976b   *Sociological Ambivalance and other Essays.* The Free Press, New York.

1977   The Sociology of Science: an episodic memoir. In *The Sociology of Science in Europe* (edited with Jerry Gaston). University of Southern Illinois Press, Carbondale. (Also issued in 1979 under the same title.)

1978   Institutionalized Altruism: the Case of the Professions (with Thomas F. Gieryn) in 1982a, pp. 109–134.

1979a   (Written by Ludwik Fleck, translated from German). *Genesis and Development of a Scientific Fact.* University of Chicago Press, Chicago.

1979b   Remembering Paul Lazarsfeld. In *Qualitative and Quantitative Research Papers in Honor of Paul F. Lazarsfeld* (edited with James S. Coleman and Peter H. Rossi). The Free Press, New York, pp. 19–22.

1980a   On the Oral Transmission of Knowledge. In Robert K. Merton and Matilda White Riley (eds.), *Sociological Traditions from Generation to Generation: Glimpses of the American Experience.* Ablex Publishing Corp., New Jersey, pp. 1–35.

1980b   Remembering the Young Talcott Parsons. *The American Sociologist*, **19** (May), 68–71.

1980c   Citation Classic: *Social Theory and Social Structure. Current Contents*, **21**, May 26, 12.

1981a   Remarks on Theoretical Pluralism. In *Continuities in Structural Inquiry* (edited by Robert K. Merton and Peter M. Blau). Sage Publications, London, pp. i–vii.

1981b   Our Sociological Vernacular. *Columbia*, 42–44. 1982a, pp. 100–106.

1982a   *Social Research and the Practising Professions* (edited by Aaron Rosenblatt and Thomas F. Gieryn). Abt Books, Cambridge.

1982b   Alvin W. Gouldner: Genesis and Growth of a Friendship. *Theory and Society*, **11**, 915–938.

1983   Florian Znaniecki: A Short Reminiscence. *Journal of the History of the Behavioural Sciences*, **10**, 123–126.

1984a   Socially Expected Durations: A Case Study of Concept Formation in Sociology. In Wallis W. Powell and Richard Robbins (eds.),

Alexander, Jeffrey, C. (1982) *Theoretical Logic in Sociology: Positivism, Presuppositions and Current Controversies*. University of California Press, California.

Allen, P.J. (ed.) (1963) *P. A. Sorokin in Review*. Duke University Press, Durham, North Carolina.

Bahr, Howard, M., Theodore, J. Johnson and M. Ray Seitz (1971) Influential Scholars and Works in the Sociology of Race and Minority Relations, 1944–1968. *American Sociologist*, **6**, 296–296.

Bain, Read (1962) The Most Important Sociologists? *American Sociological Review*, **27**, 746–748.

Baldamus, W. (1976) *The Structure of Sociological Inference*. Robertson, London.

Barbano, Filippo (1968) Social Structures and Social Functions: the Emancipation of Structural Analysis in Sociology. *Inquiry*, **II**, 40–84.

Barber, Bernard (1952) *Science and the Social Order*. The Free Press, New York.

Barber, Bernard (1975) Toward a New View of the Sociology of Knowledge. In Coser, 1975a, pp. 103–116.

Barnes, S. B. and R. G. A. Dolby (1970) The Scientific Ethos: A Deviant Viewpoint. *European Journal of Sociology*, **II**, 1–25.

Becker, George. (1984) Pietism and Science: A Critique of Robert K. Merton's Hypothesis. *American Journal of Sociology*, **89**, 1065–1090.

Ben-David, Joseph (1971) *The Scientist's Role in Society*. Prentice-Hall, New Jersey.

Ben-David, Joseph (1973) The State of Sociological Theory and the Sociological Community: a review article. *Comparative Studies in Society and History*, **15**, 448–472.

Ben-David, Joseph (1978) Emergence of National Traditions in the Sociology of Science: The United States and Great Britain. In Jerry Gaston
(ed.), *The Sociology of Science*. Jossey-Bass, San Francisco, pp.
197–218.

Bernstein, Richard J. (1976) *The Restructuring of Social and Political
Theory*. Harcourt Brace Jovanovich, New York (esp. pp. 7–18).

Biddle, Bruce (1979) *Role Theory: Expectations, Identities and Behaviors*.
Academic Press, New York.

Bierstedt, Robert (1981) *American Sociological Theory — A Critical
History*. Academic Press, New York (esp. pp. 443–504).

Blau, Peter, M. (1975a) Structural Constraints of Status Complements. In
Coser, 1975a, pp. 117–138.

Blau, Peter (ed.) (1975b) *Approaches to the Study of Social Structure*. The
Free Press, New York.

Bloom, Samuel, W. and Robert N. Wilson (1982) Patient–Practitioner
Relationships. In Freeman *et al.*, 1982, pp. 315–339.

Boudon, Raymond (1981) *The Logic of Social Action*. Routledge & Kegan
Paul, London (translated by David Silverman).

Bryant, Christopher (1976) *Sociology in Action: a critique of selected
concepts of the social role of the sociologist*. Allen & Unwin, London.

Burrell, Gibson and Gareth Morgan (1979) *Sociological Paradigms and
Organizational Analysis*. Heinemann, London.

Campbell, Colin (1982) A dubious distinction? An inquiry into the value
and use of Merton's concepts of manifest and latent function. *American Sociological Review*, **47**, 29–44.

Caplovitz, David (1977) Robert K. Merton as Editor: Review Essay.
Contemporary Sociology, **6**, 142–150.

Caplovitz, David (1983) *The Stages of Social Research*. John Wiley, New
York (esp. Chap. 16).

Clinard, Marshall B. (1964) The Theoretical Implications of Anomie and
Deviant Behavior. In Clinard, Marshall B. (ed.), *Anomie and Deviant
Behavior:a discussion and critique*. The Free Press, New York, pp.
1–56.

Cloward, Richard (1959) Illegitimate means, anomie and deviant behavior.
American Sociological Review, **24**, 164–176.

Cloward, Richard and Lloyd Ohlin (1960) *Delinquency and Opportunity*.
The Free Press, New York.

Cohen, A.K. (1959) Social Disorganization and Deviant Behavior. In
Merton *et al.*, 1959a, pp. 461–484.

Cole, Jonathan (1979) *Fair Science: Women in the Scientific Community*.
The Free Press, New York.

Cole, Jonathan and Stephen Cole (1973) *Social Stratification in Science*.
University of Chicago Press, Chicago.

185–200.

Coser, Lewis (ed.) (1975a) *The Idea of Social Structure: papers in Honor of Robert K. Merton*. Harcourt Brace Jovanovich, New York.

Coser, Lewis (1975b) Merton's Uses of the Sociological Tradition. In Coser, 1975a, pp. 85–100.

Coser, Lewis, A. (1977) *Masters of Sociological Thought (2nd edn)*. Harcourt Brace Jovanovich, New York (esp. pp. 562–567).

Coser, Lewis and Robert Nisbet (1975) Merton and the Contemporary Mind: an affectionate dialogue. In Coser, 1975a, pp. 3–10.

Coser, Lewis and Morris Rosenberg (eds.) (1964) *Sociological Theory: a book of readings* (2nd edn.) Macmillan, New York.

Coser, Rose Laub (1975) The Complexity of Roles as a Seedbed of Autonomy. In Coser, 1975a, pp. 237–264.

Current Biography (1965) Robert K. Merton. **26**, 20–23.

Cuzzort, R.P. (1969) The Unanticipated Consequences of Human Actions: the Views of Robert King Merton. In *Humanity and Modern Sociological Thought*. Holt, Rinehart & Winston, New York (esp. Chap. 4).

Dahrendorf, Ralf (1968) *Essays in the Theory of Society*. Routledge & Kegan Paul, London.

Davis, Kingsley (1948) *Human Society*. Macmillan, New York.

Davis, Kingsley (1959) The Myth of Functional Analysis as a special method in Sociology and Anthropology. *American Sociological Review*, **24**(6), 757–772.

De Lellio, Anna (1985) Socially Expected Durations: interview with Robert K. Merton. *Rassegna Italiana Di Sociologia*, **26**(1), 3–26 (in Italian).

Demerath, Nicholas, J. III (1967) Synecdoche and Structural-Functionalism. In N. J. Demerath and R. A. Peterson (eds.), *System, Change* and Conflict. The Free Press, New York, pp. 501–518.

Dore, Ronald Philip (1961) Function and Cause. American Sociological Review, **26**, 843–853.

Dubin, Robert (1959) Deviant Behaviour and Social Structure: continuities in social theory. American Sociological Review, **24**, 147–164.

Durkheim, Emile (1859–1897) Suicide. Free Press, Glencoe, Ill.

Eisenstadt, S. N. and M. Curelaru (1976) The Form of Sociology: Paradigms and Crises. John Wiley, New York.

Fenton,Steve (1984) Durkheim and Modern Sociology. Cambridge University Press, Cambridge.

Firth, Raymond (ed.) (1957) Man and Culture: an Evaluation of the Work of Malinowski. Routledge & Kegan Paul, London.

Freeman, Howard E. et al. (eds.) (1982) Handbook of Medical Sociology. Prentice-Hall, Englewood Cliffs, N.J.

Friedrichs, Robert W. (1970) A Sociology of Sociology. Free Press, New York, and Macmillan, London.

Garfield, Eugene (1977) Robert K. Merton: Among the giants. Current Contents, (11 July 1977), 5–7. (Reprinted in E. Garfield, Essays of an Information Scientist. ISI Press, Philadelphia, 1980, pp. 176–178).

Garfield, Eugene. (1980) Citation measures of the influence of Robert K. Merton. In Thomas F. Gieryn, 1980, pp. 61–74.

Gaston, Jerry (1970) Originality and Competition in Science. University of Chicago Press, Chicago.

Giddens, Anthony (1977) Functionalism: après la lutte. In Studies in Social and Political Theory. Hutchinson, London (esp. pp. 96–134).

Giddens, Anthony (1984) The Constitution of Society. Polity Press, Cambridge.

Gieryn, Thomas (ed.) (1980) Science and Social Structure: a festschrift for Robert K. Merton. The New York Academy of Sciences, New York.

Gieryn, Thomas F. (1982) Relativist/Constructivist programmes in the sociology of science: redundance and retreat. Social Studies of Science, **12**, 279–297 (see also remainder of debate in following pages).

Goode, William, J. (1973) Explorations in Social Theory. Oxford University Press, New York.

Gouldner, Alvin (1957) Cosmopolitans and Locals: towards an analysis of latent social roles Administrative Science Quarterly, **2**, 281–306, 444–480.

Gouldner, Alvin (1959) Reciprocity and Autonomy in Functional Theory. (Reprinted in Gouldner, 1973b, pp. 190–225.)

Gouldner, Alvin (1961) Anti-Minotaur: the myth of a value-free sociology. Social Problems. (Reprinted in Gouldner, 1973b, pp. 3–26.)

Press, New York.

Horton, John (1964) The Dehumanization of Anomie and Alienation: a problem in the ideology of sociology. *British Journal of Sociology*, **15**, 283–300.

Hunt, Morton, M. (1961) 'How Does It Come to Be So?' Profile of Robert K. Merton. *New Yorker*, **36**, 39–63.

Hyman, Herbert and Eleanor Singer (eds.) (1968) *Readings in Reference Group Theory and Research*. Free Press, New York.

Jackson, J.A. (ed.) (1972) *Role*. Sociological Studies 4, Cambridge University Press, Cambridge.

Johnson, Harry, M. (1960) *Sociology: a systematic introduction*. Routledge & Kegan Paul/Harcourt Brace, London.

Kendall, Patricia (1975) Theory and Research: the case of studies in medical education. In Coser, 1975a, pp. 301–322.

Knight, Frank, H. (1921) *Risk, Uncertainty and Profit*. Houghton Mifflin, Cambridge, Mass.

Knorr-Cetina, Karin D. (1982) Scientific Communities or Transepistemic Arenas of Research: a critique of quasi-economic models of science. *Social Studies of Science*, **12**(1), 101–130.

Koestler, Arthur (1973) *The Act of Creation*. Hutchinson, London.

Kolb, William L. (1958) Review of Social Theory and Social Structure. *American Journal of Sociology*, **63**, 544–555.

Kuhn, Thomas S. (1962) *The Structure of Scientific Revolutions*. University of Chicago Press, Chicago.

Kuhn, Thomas, S. (1977) *The Essential Tension*. University of Chicago Press, Chicago.

Landau, Martin (1968) On the Use of Functional Analysis in American Science. *Social Research*, **35**, 48–75.

Lazarsfeld, Paul, F. (1975) Working with Merton. In Coser, 1975a, pp. 35–66.

Lazarsfeld, Paul F. and Herbert Menzel (1961) On the Relation between Individual and Collective Properties. In Amitai Etzioni (ed.), *A Sociological Reader on Complex Organisation* (2nd. edn). Holt, Rinehart & Winston, New York, pp. 499–516.

Lemert, Edwin M. (1964) Social Structure, Social Control and Deviation in Clinard, 1964, pp. 57-97.

Levine, Donald, N., Ellwood, B. Carter and Eleanor Miller Gorman (1976) Simmel's Influence on American Sociology. *American Journal of Sociology*, **81**(4), 813–841.

Lipset, S.M. (1955) The Department of Sociology. In R. G. Hoxie *et al.* (eds.), *The History of the Faculty of Political Science at Columbia University*. Columbia University Press, New York, pp. 284–303.

Lipset, S.M. (1969a) Issues in Social Class Analysis. In *Revolution and Counter Revolution*. Heinemann, London.

Lipset, S.M. (1969b) From Socialism to Sociology. In Irving Louis Horowitz (ed.), *Sociological Self-Images*. Sage, California, pp. 143–176.

Lipset, S.M. and A. Basu (1975) Intellectual Types and Political Roles. In Coser, 1975a, pp. 433–470.

Loomis, Charles P. and Zona K. Loomis (1965) *Modern Social Theories* (2nd. edn.) Van Nostrand, New York (esp. Chap. 5, pp. 246–326).

Lukes, Steven (1973) *Emile Durkheim: his life and work*. Penguin, London.

MacIver, Robert (1968) *As a Tale that is Told*. University of Chicago Press, Chicago.

March, James G. and Herbert A. Simon (1958) *Organizations*. John Wiley, New York (esp. pp. 37–47).

Martindale, Don (1979) *The Nature and Types of Sociological Theory*. Routledge & Kegan Paul, London (esp. pp. 425–427, 471–476).

Matza, David (1969) *Becoming Deviant*. Prentice-Hall, Englewood Cliffs, New Jersey (esp. pp. 57–62, 96–99).

Menzies, Ken (1982) *Sociological Theory in Use*. Routledge & Kegan Paul, London.

Miles, Mary Wilson (1975) Bibliography — Robert K. Merton, 1934–1975. In Coser, 1975a.

Miles, Mary Wilson (1985). Publications since 1975 (manuscript).

Mills, C. Wright (1959) *The Sociological Imagination*. Oxford University Press, Oxford.

Mitroff, Ian I. (1974) Norms and Counter-norms in a Select Group of the

in Seventeenth Century England. *American Journal of Sociology*, **78**, 223–231.

Oromaner, Mark J. (1968) The Most Cited Sociologists: an analysis of introductory text citations. *American Sociologist*, **3**, 124–126.

Oromaner, Mark J. (1970) Comparison of Influentials in Contemporary American and British Sociology. *British Journal of Sociology*, **13**, 324–332.

Oromaner, Mark J. (1980) Influentials in Sociological Textbooks and Journals, 1955 and 1970. *The American Sociologist*, **15**, 169–174.

Page, Charles (1982) *Fifty Years in the Sociological Enterprise*. University of Massachusetts Press, Amhurst.

Parsons, Talcott (1937) *The Structure of Social Action*. The Free Press, New York.

Parsons, Talcott (1951) *The Social System*. The Free Press, New York (esp. pp. 256–267, 321–325).

Parsons, Talcott (1975) The Present Status of Structural-Functional Theory in Sociology. In Coser, 1975a, pp. 67-84.

Perrucci, Robert (1980) Sociology and the Introductory Textbook. *American Sociologist*, **15**, 39–49.

Persell, Caroline Hodges (1984) An interview with Robert K. Merton. *Teaching Sociology*, **11**(4), 470–486.

Pinder, Craig and Larry Moore (eds.) (1980) *Middle Range Theory and the Study of Organizations*. Martinus Nijhoff, Boston.

Restivo, Sal (1983) The Myth of the Kuhnian Revolution. *Sociological Theory*, **1983**, Jossey–Bass, San Francisco, pp. 293–305.

Riley, Matilda White (1963) *Sociological Research*. Harcourt, Brace and World, New York.

Room, Robin (1976) Ambivalence as a Sociological Explanation: the case of cultural explanations of alcohol problems. *American Sociological Review*, **41**, 1047–1065.

Shils, Edward (1970) *The Calling of Sociology*. University of Chicago Press, Chicago.

Simon, William and John H.Gagnon (1976) The Anomie of Affluence: a post-Mertonian conception. *American Journal of Sociology*, **82**, 356–378.

Snizek, William, Ellsworth Fuhrman and Michael Miller (eds.) (1979) *Contemporary Issues in Theory and Research*. Aldwych Press, London.

Sorokin. P.A. (1966) *Sociological Theories of Today*. Harper & Row, New York (esp. pp. 445–456).

Stehr, Nico (1978) The Ethos of Science Revisited: social and cognitive norms. In Jerry Gaston (ed.) *The Sociology of Science*. Jossey-Bass, San Francisco, pp. 172–196.

Stinchcombe, Arthur (1968) *Constructing Social Theories*. Harcourt, Brace and World, New York.

Stinchcombe, Arthur (1975) Merton's Theory of Social Structure. In Coser, 1975a, pp. 11–34.

Stinchcombe, Arthur (1978) *Theoretical Methods in Social History*. Academic Press, New York.

Storer, Norman (1966) *The Social System of Science*. Holt, Rinehart & Winston, New York.

Storer, Norman (1973) Introduction and Prefatory Notes. In Robert K. Merton, *The Sociology of Science*.

Sztompka, Piotr (1974) *System and Function*. Academic Press, New York.

Sztompka, Piotr (1986) *Robert K. Merton: an Intellectual Profile*. Macmillan, London.

Taylor, Laurie (1971) *Deviance and Society*. Michael Joseph, London.

Taylor, Ian, Paul Walton and Jock Young (1973) *The New Criminology*. Routledge & Kegan Paul (esp. pp. 91–110).

Thio, A. (1975) A Critical Look at Merton's Anomie Theory. *Pacific Sociological Review*, **18**, 139–158.

Turner, Brian (1981) *For Weber: essays on the Sociology of fate*. Routledge & Kegan Paul, Boston.

Turner, Jonathan H. (1974) *The Structure of Sociological Theory*. Dorsey Press, Homewood, Illinois (esp. Chap. 4).

Turner, Jonathan H. (1985) Unanswered questions in the convergence between structuralist and interactionist role theories. In S. N. Eisenstadt and H. J. Helle (eds.) *Perspectives on Micro-Sociological Theory*. Sage Publications, London, pp. 22–36.

Wilson, John (1983) *Social Theory*. Prentice-Hall, N.J.

Wrong, Denis (1961) The Oversocialized Conception of Man in Modern Sociology. *The American Sociological Review*, **26**, 184–193.

Wunderlich, R. (1979) The Scientific Ethos: a clarification. *British Journal of Sociology*, **25**, 373–377.

Young, Jock (1974) New Directions in Sub-cultural Theory. In John Rex (ed.), *Approaches to Sociology: an introduction to major trends in British Sociology*. Routledge & Kegan Paul, London, pp. 160–186.

Zeitlin, Irving M. (1968) *Ideology and the Development of Sociological Theory*. Prentice-Hall, N.J.

Zetterberg, H. (1965) *On Theory and Verification in Sociology* (3rd edn). Bedminister Press, N.J. (first ed., 1954).

Zuckerman, Harriet (1976) *Scientific Elite*. University of Chicago Press, Chicago.

Zuckerman, Harriet (1978) Deviant Behavior and Social Control in Science. In Edward Sargin (ed.), *Deviance and Social Change*. Sage Publications, London, pp. 87–138.

Zuckerman, Harriet (1979) Theory Choice and Problem Choice in Science. In Jerry Gaston (ed.), *The Sociology of Science*. Jossey-Bass, San Francisco, pp. 65–95.

Index